Western Canada in tl

International Econor

Western Canada in the International Economy

Edward J. Chambers

Michael B. Percy

Publication No. 2 in
Western Studies in Economic Policy
Edward J. Chambers, Series Editor

A joint series of the
Western Centre for Economic Research
at the University of Alberta
and the C. D. Howe Institute

The University of Alberta Press

This edition published by
The University of Alberta Press
Athabasca Hall
Edmonton, Alberta
Canada T6G 2E8

Copyright © The University of Alberta Press 1992

ISBN 0-88864-247-4 paper

Canadian Cataloguing in Publication Data

Chambers, Edward J.
Western Canada in the international economy

(Western studies in economic policy ; no. 2)
Includes bibliographical references.
ISBN 0-88864-247-4

1. Canada, Western—Foreign economic relations.
2. Canada, Western—Commerce. 3. Canada, Western—
Economic conditions. I. Percy, Michael, 1948–
II. Title. III. Series
HF3226.5.C52 1992   337.712   C92-091427-6

Printed by Printing Services, University of Alberta, Edmonton,
Alberta, Canada

C ontents

Figures & Charts

T ables

Preface

The original suggestion and the early initiatives for this research came from Dr. Brian Scarfe when he was the Director of the Western Centre for Economic Research. The study examines the place of Western Canada and each of the four provinces in the global marketplace, a marketplace instrumental in developing the region and in generating high levels of per capita income for its residents. The study comes at a time when prospective changes in the Canadian constitution are being negotiated, and when there is increasing evidence that Western Canada must find its place in a newly emerging world of major trading blocs. The combination of internal and external circumstances pose a challenge not only to policymakers in Western Canada, but also to the private sector, particularly in the resource-based industries of the region, for it is the agricultural and non-agricultural resource sectors that have defined Western Canada's international competitiveness over many decades. We hope the research presented here serves to clarify the strategic options that face the West in the face of rapid technological change affecting both product demands and input combinations in the resource sector, environmental concerns, and continuing questions about the impact of volatile commodity prices and markets on the region's welfare.

Thomas E. Kierans,
President and Chief Executive Officer
C.D. Howe Institute

Edward J. Chambers, Director
Western Centre for Economic
Research

Acknowledgements

The Western Centre for Economic Research would like to thank the following for grants in support of publication costs for this study: the Winspear Foundation, Imperial Oil, NOVA Corporation, Potash Corporation of Saskatchewan, Banister Continental, Maclab Enterprises, Bumper Development Corporation, Chieftain International, Husky Oil, and Alberta Energy.

I ntroduction

Introduction

What are Western Canada's present competitive strengths as defined by the region's position in international export markets? Will these strengths remain the same in the next generation? If they shift, how and in what degree will they be altered? In this era of globalization it is important that the region's position in international markets, particularly the composition and direction of its exports, be more widely understood. A good working knowledge of the present trading links of Western Canada, and each of its four provinces with the United States, with the Pacific rim, with Europe, and with other countries is a necessary foundation to identifying the range of actions in both the private and public sectors necessary to maintain the quality of life presently characterizing this part of the world. Change is ever present whether in technology, in demography, in market conditions, in socio-political movements and public policies of important trading partners, or in concerns over the state of the physical environment. The force of these changes can impact the living standards that we enjoy. Reactive strategies for coping with change will no longer suffice; they are more than likely to lead to decline and eventually to demise. The challenge for Western Canada is to take advantage of these shifting patterns, but if that is impossible then at least to foster the realistic capability of positive responses to signals of change.

The work is divided into four parts. The first provides the necessary situational assessment of the region. For this purpose we have assembled a series of employment and trade profiles for the region and each of its four provinces. Comparisons of the industrial composition of employment in the west, in the four provinces, and in Canada as a whole, show how human resources are deployed. This chapter on profiles also identifies the relative and absolute importance of merchandise export trade, its commodity composition, and the geographic markets where customers are located. The empirical evidence points to some important conclusions with significant consequence for the Western Canadian economy. Employment in the west in primary industries- agricultural and nonagricultural- is relatively high, and the market conditions facing these industries remain a major determinant of regional economic performance and welfare. The narrowness of the regional export base with its marked dependence on raw materials is apparent in the fact that more than one half of merchandise exports are accounted for by only six commodities. This export base concentration is shared by three of the four provinces with only the Manitoba profile displaying some measurable degree of diversification. The situational analysis also reveals that the country markets for Western Canadian exports are rather different from those of the country as a whole, and that geographic export markets differ quite sharply for each of the provinces.

In the second chapter some important measures of instability in the Western Canadian economy are reported and their consequences considered. This section of the monograph conveys new evidence on the experience of the western economy over the past generation. The information includes an export value weighted index of commodity prices composed of the region's principal exports. It also reports an exchange rate based measure of the competitiveness of the most important exports from the Western Canadian economy. The instrument used for this evaluation is a newly constructed index of real and effective exchange rates made up of a twenty country currency basket. The index weights take account not only of the value of direct export trade with each of the nineteen countries in each commodity, but they also incorporate a factor reflecting the competition Western Canadian exports face in the markets of others within the designated currency basket. What emerges from the analysis is a picture of economic instability in Western Canada driven by the effects of commodity price fluctuations on the performance of business and the expectations of households. Commodity price instability has been aggravated by the behaviour of the exchange rate which during much of the past generation has been procyclical in its effects on Western Canada, depreciating during periods of rising commodity prices and appreciating during phases of commodity price increases. The chapter casts doubt that Canada is an optimal currency area, leads to skepticism about the effects of a floating exchange rate in moderating regional instability, and asks if the west would have better served in the past two decades by an exchange rate pegged to the American dollar.

The next section of the book turns first to some of the buffers that are available in the region to assuage the effects of economic instability. These range from agricultural support programs, to provincial government royalty rate adjustments, to collaborative marketing efforts by private producers. However, these buffers, many of the largest of which require actions by public authorities and interregional income transfers to alleviate the problems of instability, are scarcely the whole story.

Buffers may lead to a state of dependency rather than facilitating necessary transitions. The world is changing, and the industries in which Western Canada has enjoyed a comparative advantage are at risk to technological change. The examples are many; from the results of material science in bringing about substitutes for wood products and metals, to the impacts of bio-technology on crop production in countries that have been important export markets, to the growing importance of forest plantations in parts of the world whose climate allows measurably higher annual tree growth rates than are possible in the west. Further Western Canada, as we are now well aware, is not immune to the demands of the environmental movement, nor to strategies of LDCs that rely on natural resource exploitation as a principal avenue to higher levels of per capita income. Western Canada as a resource producer will also be affected by changes that follow from the death of communism in eastern Europe. These will certainly lead to a greater utilization of the abundant agricultural and nonagricultural resource base in that part of the world. Against this backdrop the chapter examines the options facing the private sector and the kind of adjustments that will be demanded. For Western Canada the implicit industrial strategy of being a low cost producer of undifferentiated commodity products may no longer suffice. In summary the questions are what private sector strategies must be considered for bringing about changes in the export base status quo, and what role should governments play in facilitating the transition.

The final chapter is directed at the important question of the effects of trade liberalization on structural change in Western Canada. The international trading environment in recent years has been one of increasing turbulence, despite evidence of freer trade within regional blocs such as the European Economic Community and the more recent Canada - United States Free Trade Agreement. The chapter begins by recognizing the contribution of the Canadian economic union to a regional economy which remains natural resource dependent. But it is also clear that freer trading arrangements with other countries that serve to increase the size of available markets bestow important benefits. Advantages to Western Canada would follow from successful completion of the Uruguay round of GATT negotiations, in particular the reduction of agricultural subsidies and improved market access for natural resource based products. A range of non-tariff trade barriers and the lack of visibility in import controls have inhibited attempts in the region at value added and the diversification of the export base. Trade liberalization is therefore of great importance to Western Canada.

The chapter also considers the impact of the FTA on Western Canada and concludes that the total effect of the agreement will neither be as beneficial as proclaimed by advocates, nor as dire as suggested by opponents. The most significant long term positive impact is likely to come from a successful conclusion to negotiations over a common definition of what constitutes a subsidy. Attention is also given to the effect on the region of a wider North American agreement including Mexico, and to the effects of Europe 1992. The effects on Western Canadian producers of a tripartite North American agreement would depend very much on the application of similar rules for both Canadian and Mexican access to the American market. The EEC already has significant non-tariff barriers on agricultural and other resource based imports. The question is whether they will be reinforced or reduced by integration.

We turn first to identifying key economic profiles.

1 Profiles

Economists have long studied the behaviour of nation states. Although these units are integral components of a total world economic system, they are ordinarily thought to have some independence of policy action. But as globalization occurs with closely coupled trade and financial linkages, single "nation state" economies cannot be isolated from world market forces. This is even more evident for vast geographic regions such as Western Canada whose economy is one small island in the total world archipelago. Interdependencies abound; a global perspective seems the only sensible one to apply.

The Western Canadian economy and that of each of the four provinces composing it, have from the earliest stages of their development enjoyed significant commodity, finance, and human resource links with the broader international economy. Our concern in this monograph is primarily with contemporary trade, or commodity linkages, but this trade-based production required much capital investment, a significant portion of which was funded from foreign sources. Many observers note that the internal operating systems necessary for the region's participation in the world economy encompass high levels of capital goods per employee and a transport and communication infrastructure both massive and complex, so that, in fact, Western Canada bears many similarities to a traditional resource-based economy enjoying high levels of per capita income. Further, the unquestioned place of immigration in early Western Canadian development is well known. The pre-1914 era of settlement involving migration to Western Canada of hundreds of thousands from overseas, from Central Canada and the Maritimes, and from the United States remains the most dramatic period in almost a century and a half of Canadian economic history. However, in this monograph we will not deal directly with the role of capital flows, nor with the contribution of immigration to Western Canada. That is another story for another time. Rather, we focus on the trading links, particularly the export links of the region as a whole and each of the four provinces (Manitoba, Saskatchewan, Alberta and British Columbia) with the global economy. What are the main exports of the region and each of the provinces? What are the spatial markets for these exports? How do the prices of these exports move cyclically and secularly? How do these price movements compare with those in broad measures of the price level such as the Consumer Price Index? To what degree do movements in the Bank of Canada's G-10 exchange rate index ameliorate/amplify commodity price swings? How do movements in an index of effective exchange rates for Western Canada compare with those in the national index? What challenges to Western Canada's export base grow out of emerging developments in the international economy, including the North American Free Trade Agreement, the increased economic power of Pacific Rim countries, Europe of 1992, the aspirations of the LDCs and NICs, the environmental movement, and the evidence of managed rather than free trade? The answers to these questions do much to explain Western Canada's current economic position, its long standing political concerns, and its viable future options.

This chapter begins with a summary of job distributions in each of the four provinces and Western Canada as a whole, in order to provide an overview of the similarities and differences in the industrial allocation of labour between the provinces and with the national economy. This is followed by a discussion of major commodity exports, the export profile of each province, and the major spatial markets for the provinces and the region, to identify the region's export base and to draw out contrasts between these markets and those for Canadian exports as a whole. This analysis will suggest the difficulties of evaluating Western Canada as a homogeneous regional entity.

Demography also reveals provincial differences. Though the proportion of the Canadian population residing in the west increased from 26.5% in 1971 to 28.9% in 1990, the differences in the experience of the four provinces during these years are substantial and readily apparent in the fact that some

72% of Western Canada's population resided in British Columbia and Alberta in 1990 compared with only 66% in 1971. In each province there are entirely different sets of market opportunities and clearly distinguishable types of problems in areas of rapid as opposed to slow, population growth. Aggregate differences are further complicated by age profile differences, for example as between Alberta and British Columbia, that affect household demand, the needs for public facilities, types of housing, the stability of income flows, and the availability of labour.

The Industrial Composition of Employment

Chart 1. 1(a) shows the percentage shares of industrial distribution of employment by major category in 1988 for each of the four provinces in Western Canada. To permit comparisons, the distribution for Western Canada is compared in Chart I. 1(b) with that for the country as a whole. The most important points of contrast between the four western provinces and with the national are:

1. The share of employment in agriculture is 6.9%, or approximately twice the national average.

2. Those with jobs in nonagricultural primary industries (mining, including oil and gas exploration and development, forestry and fishing) amount to 4.1% of total employment compared with a national figure of 2.5%.

3. Perhaps most importantly, only 10.1% of jobs are in manufacturing compared with 17.2% nationally and more than 25% in Ontario.

4. Generally the distribution of jobs in other industries (construction, transportation and utilities, services, and public administration) closely resembles the national average.

The charts comparing employment across the four provinces point to an important conclusion: differences between provinces, even between the three prairie provinces themselves, are quite as striking as the differences between Western Canada and the country as a whole. Most obvious are differences in the relative importance of agriculture, other extractive industries, and manufacturing. Agriculture's relative importance in Saskatchewan is more than twice as great as in Alberta and Manitoba, and these two provinces, in turn, have more than twice the proportion of their labour force on the farm compared with British Columbia. While in all provinces the proportion in non-agricultural primary industries exceeds the national, the Alberta figure, driven by the energy industry, is measurably higher than the other three. More generally, in Saskatchewan and Alberta the primary resource sectors

Chart 1.1(a): Provincial Employment by Industry

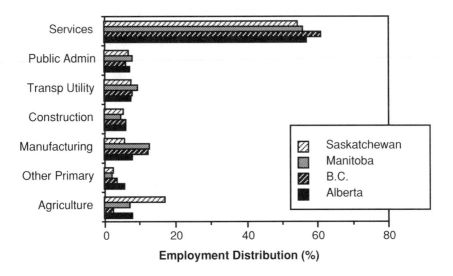

Chart 1.1(b): Western Canada vs Canada Employment

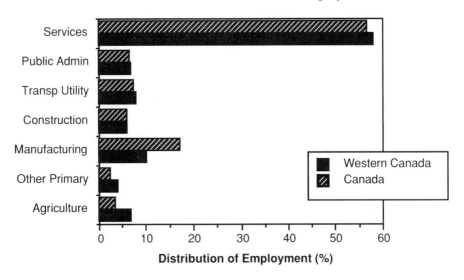

Source: Statistics Canada, *The Labour Force.*

accounted in 1988 for 19.9 and 13.8% of all jobs, while in Manitoba and British Columbia the percentages were 9.5 and 6.3% respectively.

Finally, the greater relative importance of manufacturing activity in Manitoba and British Columbia is readily apparent though, even in these cases, it is some five share points below the national average and some twelve percentage points below the share of manufacturing employment in Ontario. Further understanding of the differences in manufacturing activity in these two provinces is gained from a recent study of the Economic Council of Canada (Postner and Wesa 1985). The authors classified manufacturing in terms of primary, secondary, and local activities, and found that on average over the years between 1975 and 1983 more than one in every two jobs in British Columbia were in primary manufacturing activities, i.e., in the initial processing of raw materials. This is in contrast to Manitoba where well over one half of manufacturing industry employment was in secondary manufacturing, i.e., activities more oriented toward finished goods production and heavily dependent on a stable and experienced work force.

Presenting the industrial composition of employment as we have above may lead the reader to conclude that resource industries are less important in the west than is generally believed. Therefore it is important to recognize that industrial profiles do not tell the whole story, in particular they do not tell the indirect and induced effects on the provincial economies of the resource-based industries. Indirect effects represent the linkages with other sectors of the economy where the outputs of those sectors, including the outputs of professional services, are necessary inputs to the production of the resource industries. Induced effects represent the spin-off employment effects of spending by those employed in resource extraction or processing. The provincial input-output tables of Statistics Canada indicate that as much as one-third or more of provincial employment is accounted for by the sum of the direct, indirect, and induced effects of export industry activity in British Columbia, at least, and likely more in Alberta, and Saskatchewan. As we shall see below, the exports of these provinces are heavily resource based.

Western Canada's Merchandise Trade Links with the Global Economy

We now want to identify the share of Canadian exports originating in the region, and to report Western Canada's merchandise trade links with the global economy in terms of specific commodities. There is some risk in focussing on exports rather than on total trade because the story of trading links is obviously less than complete. While there is little reason to believe *a priori* that items constituting the material living standard of households in

Table 1.1: Western Canada's Share in Total Merchandise Exports, 1986-89

Year	Western Canada Exports ($mill.)	Canada Exports ($mill.)	Western Canada Export Share (%)
1986	30,695.4	116,733.4	26.3
1987	36,255.1	121,462.3	29.8
1988	39,112.1	133,904.0	29.2
1989	38,163.3	133,483.0	28.6

Data on export values are in current dollars.

Source: Adapted from Statistics Canada, *Exports by Country* (65-003) and *Provincial Economic Accounts: Annual Estimates* (13-213)

Western Canada have measurably different import content from those in other households, it is far from clear that given the different industrial base in Western Canada intermediate import requirements will be identical to those of Canadian business generally. However, there is purpose in the focus on merchandise exports to other countries since it is these shipments that have secured the region's role in the world economy. This analysis is based on trade data for the latter years of the eighties as reported by Statistics Canada, much of which has been collated by provincial government agencies in the four provinces. Since mid-1984 Statistics Canada has reported exports by province of origin defined as the province in which the commodity exported was grown, extracted, or exported. Prior to that time provincial origin data was not really adapted to this type of evaluation since exports were reported on a bill of lading basis (indicating the province in which merchandise was last placed on board a carrier for export).

Table 1.1 shows the relationship between total exports from Western Canada and total Canadian exports and provides evidence of the region's contribution to total foreign shipments.

In current dollar values, Western Canada's exports were some 29% of national exports in the late 1980s. The increased relative share in 1987, largely is the result of improved nonagricultural commodity prices, particularly in 1987 compared with their 1986 levels.

The Region's Export Profile

Table 2.1 is a profile of the region's major export categories by Harmonized System code of commodity classification for the 1986-89 years. The right hand column contains the percentage share of total Western Canadian exports contained in each category. Perhaps the most striking feature of the table is that six commodity grade products amount to more than one-half of

Table 2.1: Top Tier Western Canadian Merchandise Exports
(1986-89 average)

Commodity	% Share of total exports
Crude petroleum (27.09)	11.73
Sawn softwood lumber (44.07)	11.08
Woodpulp (47)	9.29
Wheat (10.01)	8.04
Natural gas (27.11.21)	7.59
Coal (27.01)	5.11
Newsprint (48.01)	2.75
Potash (31.04)	2.48
Copper ores and concentrates (26.03)	1.98
Sulphur (25.03)	1.82
Fish (3)	1.51
Canola (12.05)	1.40
Aluminum (76)	1.39
Paperboard (48-48.01)	1.38
Total	**67.55**

Source: Statistics Canada, *Exports by Country* (65-003)

total export values. These commodities are crude oil, commodity grade woodpulp, sawn construction lumber, natural gas, wheat, and coal. With this degree of concentration, simultaneous slumps in forest product and energy markets cast a pall over the region, while favourable market conditions generate a "boom" atmosphere. Of course, if slumps and booms in particular sectors are offsetting, then diversification in resource industries helps stabilize the regional economy though not necessarily that of each province.

Even extending the list to 23 beyond the top six exports leaves few more differentiated products. The table shows the dramatic dependence on natural resource trade. Two farm commodities – wheat and canola – are among the top dozen export products. Among other commodities, potash, newsprint, copper ores, paper and paperboard, fish, aluminum, and sulphur generate large dollar flows. Additional exports, included in the 23 other groups and made up largely of commodity grade materials, are found in Table 3.1. A major criterion for inclusion in the "second tier" list is that export shares should have exceeded 1% in at least one of the four years. In the group there

Table 3.1: Second Tier Western Canadian Merchandise Exports
by harmonized system classification (1986-1989 Averages)

Commodity	% of Exports
Barley (10.03)	.97
Polyethylene resins (39.01)	1.01
Hydrocarbons and derivatives (29.01 - 29.04)	.89
Other petroleum and coal products (27.11)	1.06
Alcohols and derivatives (29.05 - 29.08)	.95
Electricity (27.16)	.51
Uranium ore (28.44)	.36
Zinc (79)	.82
Live animals (1)	.90
Wood products higher value added (44.08 - 44.20)	1.50
Vehicles excluding rail (87)	1.33
Machinery and mechanical appliances* (84)	1.91
Total	**10.71**

* This category includes aircraft, including engines and parts, agricultural machinery, motor engines and other parts, ships, assembled vehicles, and boats.

Source: Statistics Canada, *Export by Country* (65-003)

is one agricultural commodity: barley. Other items including polyethylene resins, hydrocarbons, and other petroleum and coal products, as well as electricity exports, are directly related to the energy industry. Also found are some higher value added wood products (44.14 to 44.20), machinery and mechanical appliances (84), and nonrail vehicles (87). Yet together these categories of more differentiated products account for less than $50 of every $1000 in export values.

In general Tables 2.1 and 3.1 underscore Western Canada's role as an exporter of raw or partially processed materials, undifferentiated by product attribute, and with limited value added. The Western Canadian share in world production and exports assembled from a variety of sources, for several of the region's important agricultural and nonagricultural commodity exports, is in Table 4.1. The evidence is that, excepting potash, sulphur, and natural gas relative to the United States market, the region accounts for a relatively small share of world production. However, for a number of these commodities it is an international player, a keen competitor for sales in the international market place. The range of Western Canadian competitors in international export sales is considerable. In wood and paper products, competition with producers in the United States, Sweden, Finland, Portugal, Austria, and Japan is strong; in copper and zinc the United States, Australia, Peru, Mexico, Chile, Bolivia, Zaire, Zambia, South Africa, and Spain are important competitors. In the case of agricultural products, there is intense competition with the United States, Argentina, Australia, and members of the EEC. Competition in potash markets is primarily with the former Soviet Union, East and West Germany, Israel, Jordan, France, and the United States. In the case of natural gas sales to the United States, the competition is almost exclusively with American producers, though there exists potential competition with PEMEX (the Mexican national producer) and latent competition with liquid natural gas in eastern United States markets. In the case of coal, Western Canadian producers compete with Australia, the United States, South Africa, West Germany, Poland, and the Soviet Union and with domestic producers in numerous European markets. Perhaps the most important point is that there is not simply competition with domestic producers in those markets into which Canadian producers ship, but at least equally important is the head-to-head competition with "third countries" in these respective markets.

The Four Provinces: Merchandise Links with the Global Economy
Turning from the region as a whole to each province we will address three questions:

1. How important are merchandise exports to provincial Gross Domestic Product?

2.. What is the commodity profile of merchandise exports originating in each of the four provinces?

3. What are the geographical markets for these products?

Provincial governments are the most important public decision centres in the region making it necessary to consider data not simply for regional exports, but also to provide information about how each provincial economy is coupled through export trade to the larger international community. It is also important to identify the spatial or geographic markets both aggregatively and for the dominant exports of each province. For example, about 75% of Canadian merchandise exports find their way directly to the United States market. How do shipments from the region and from each of the provinces compare? Is the relative importance of particular markets for the exports of each of the four provinces similar to or distinguishable from the national, and in what degree?

Table 4.1: Western Canada's Shares of World Production and Exports:
Selected Commodities

Commodity	% Share of Production	% Share of Exports
Copper ores and conc.	5	9
Natural gas	5	5 *
Crude oil	2	8 *
Sawn and planed lumber	10	38
Paper and paperboard	1	4
Woodpulp	3	14
Sulphur (all forms)	12	45
Zinc ores and conc.	11	11
Potash	25	40
Wheat	5	20
Rapeseed	17	43
Barley	8	24

*Represents percent share of the United States market

Sources:

Copper: Data on Canadian and world production and exports of copper ores and concentrates from UNCTAD, Commodity Yearbook 1987, and the U.S. Bureau of Mines, *Minerals Yearbook,1987;* Western Canada production from Energy, Mines and Resources, *Statistical Summary of the Mineral Industry in Canada 1987,* Table 5; Western Canadian exports from Statistics Canada, *Exports by Country* (65-003)

Crude Oil: Data on Canadian and world production from OECD, *Annual Oil and Gas Statistics, 1985, 1986.* and United States import data from OECD, *Imports by Commodity* 1986 and 1987.

Natural Gas: Data on Canadian and world production, and on imports from Canada as a share of the the U.S. market from OECD, *Annual Oil and Gas Statistics, 1985, and 1986.*

Sawn and planed lumber (coniferous): Data on Canadian and world production and exports from FAO, *Yearbook of Forest Products 1984;* Western Canadian production estimated from Statistics Canada, *Sawmills and Planing Mills and Shingle Mills 1984* (35-204): Western Canadian exports from Statistics Canada, *Exports by Country* (65-003).

Newsprint: Data on Canadian and world production and exports from FAO, *Yearbook of Forest Products 1984;* Western Canadian production estimated from Statistics Canada, *Pulp and Paper Industries 1984* (36-204); Western Canadian exports from Statistics Canada, *Exports by Country* (65-003).

Woodpulp: Data on world and Canadian chemical woodpulp production from FAO, *Yearbook of Forest Products 1984;* Western Canadian production estimated from Statistics Canada, *Pulp and Paper Industries 1984* (36-204). Western Canadian exports from Statistics Canada, *Exports by Province* (36-204).

Paperboard: Data on Canadian and world production and exports from FAO, *Yearbook of Forest Products 1984;* Western Canadian exports estimated from share of Western Canadian value added in Canadian paperboard production in Statistics Canada , *Pulp and Paper Industries 1984,* (36-204).

Table 4.1 sources (continued)

Sulphur: Data on Canadian and world production and exports from UNCTAD, *Commodity Yearbook 1987*. Data on Western Canadian exports from Statistics Canada, *Exports by Country* (65-003).

Zinc: Data on world and Canadian production of ores and concentrates and alloys from U.S. Bureau of Mines, *Minerals Yearbook 1987*. Data on Western Canadian exports from Statistics Canada, *Exports by Country* (65-003).

Potash: Data on Canadian and world production and exports from United States, Bureau of Mines, *Minerals Yearbook 1987*, Volume I.

Wheat: Data on Canadian and world production and exports from FAO, *Yearbook of Agricultural Production, 1988* and FAO, *Yearbook of Trade and Commerce in Agricultural Products 1988*.

Rapeseed/Canola: Data on Canadian and world production and exports from FAO, *Yearbook of Agricultural Production 1988*, and FAO, *Yearbook of Agricultural Trade and Commerce 1988.*

Exports Relative to Provincial GDP

How important are exports relative to a standard measure of provincial output? Goods shipped beyond the borders of any province may have either a domestic or a foreign destination. Table 5.1 contains two export ratios: the first is derived from an estimate of total out of province shipments (domestic and foreign), and the second is from shipments to foreigners. The table summarizes for each province the relation of total goods exports and goods exports to foreign countries from 1986 through 1989, and to Gross Provincial Product (GPP). Total export ratios range from just over 30% in the case of Manitoba to slightly more than 40% in the case of Saskatchewan. While some caution must be used in interpreting this table, it is indicative of differences in the domestic links of each of the provinces. For example, while total British Columbia exports amounted to some 33 cents per dollar of GPP, some 24 cents, or about two-thirds, were accounted for by sales to foreigners. In contrast, Alberta exports were about equally divided between foreign sales and those to the rest of Canada.

In the case of Manitoba, interprovincial exports were considerably more important than international exports. It is clear that there is considerable variation across provinces in the relative importance of foreign markets and interprovincial markets as destinations for the direct exports of each provincial economy. With respect to domestic markets, data for the mid-eighties show the importance in Western Canada of exports to adjacent provinces [Department of Finance, *Quarterly Economic Review*, March 1991]. British Columbia's largest domestic customer is Alberta. Alberta's interprovincial exports, though dominated by shipments to Ontario and a lesser extent Quebec, are nevertheless composed of substantial flows to British Columbia and Saskatchewan. Manitoba and Saskatchewan's merchandise shipments to the other western provinces were just about equal

Table 5.1: Commodity Exports: Total Out of Province Exports and Exports to
Foreign Countries as a Share of Provincial GDP
(Annual averages 1986-1989)

Province	Foreign exports as a % of GPP	Total exports as a % of GPP
British Columbia	24.5	33.1
Alberta	19.5	39.0
Saskatchewan	27.4	40.4
Manitoba	13.4	30.4

Source: Statistics Canada, *Provincial Economic Accounts: Annual Estimates*, (13-213) *Exports by Country* (65-003); total exports from the economic accounts of the respective provinces.

in importance to those to Ontario. Given the fact that western provinces export products with low value to weight ratios the significance of market proximity is apparent.

Major Commodity Exports by Province

Table 6.1, reporting estimates of the 1986-89 annual averages, demonstrates the highly specialized commodity export base of the three western-most provinces. In each of Saskatchewan, Alberta, and British Columbia six raw materials and/or commodity grade manufactured items amounted to from two-thirds to three-quarters of the value of total provincial export shipments to foreigners. With such narrowly specialized export bases economic conditions in these units are highly sensitive to income and price shocks, a matter which we address in the next chapter. Further, the dependence of their governments on stumpage and royalties exposes provincial budgets to the hazards of potentially large annual swings in tax-expenditure balances [Smith, 1990]. Manitoba is the outlier among the four provinces, with the ranking six exports representing 46.2% of foreign shipments. The fact is that Manitoba's export base is (i) relatively diversified, and (ii) contains products with greater value added content. In British Columbia there is value added to raw materials, particularly forest resources, where much of the manufacturing work force is engaged in their conversion to construction materials, or into processed intermediate inputs themselves subject to further processing by foreign customers. However, more than 90% of forest product exports are characterized as low value added.

Table 6.1: Leading Six Commodity Exports as a Per Cent
of Total Foreign Exports by Province (1986-89 averages)

	% of foreign exports
Alberta	
Crude petroleum	26.9
Natural gas	20.8
Sulphur	5.2
Wheat	5.0
Coal	3.3
Polyethylene	2.9
Total	**64.1**
British Columbia	
Sawn and planed lumber	23.6
Woodpulp	17.8
Coal	9.0
Newsprint	5.8
Copper ore and concentrates	4.4
Paper and paperboard	2.4
Total	**63.0**
Manitoba	
Wheat	17.4
Machinery and mechanical appliances	11.2
Vehicles excluding rail	7.7
Flax	3.8
Canola	3.3
Live animals	2.8
Total	**46.2**
Saskatchewan	
Wheat	33.8
Potash	17.0
Crude petroleum	15.9
Canola	4.6
Woodpulp	3.1
Barley	2.5
Total	**76.9**

Source: Statistics Canada. Exports by Country (65-003)

In Alberta, energy exports dominate, but in Saskatchewan, wheat is primary, though shipments of potash and crude oil were in total about equal to wheat . Unlike the profiles of Manitoba and British Columbia, the major exports of these two provinces can properly be placed in the crude materials category with little in value added content, a fact underlying the smaller share of their respective labour forces in manufacturing.

A Comparison of Spatial Markets

Table 7.1 contains a summary of the spatial or geographic distribution of export markets for each province, for Western Canada as a whole, and for Canada. Figures in the table are aggregated across all commodities and represent per cent market shares derived from 1986-88 annual averages. When combined with Appendix A containing information on the spatial markets for major commodities, the table reveals the contrast in geographic markets for Western Canadian exports compared with the national, the differences in the geographic destination of shipments from each of the four provinces, and the importance of particular spatial markets for specific commodities.

An important difference in the geographic destination of Western Canadian exports compared to Canadian exports is the smaller relative importance of the American market, and the larger relative importance of Japan and other Pacific Rim countries. For Western Canada the value of shipments to the United States market represented some 54% of total shipments compared with a national figure of 75%. The figure may be surprisingly low in light of the support given by western provincial governments to the FTA based on easier export access to the United States market. However, Appendix A indicates that the aggregate figure is tempered by the vast importance of the United States market for western nonagricultural commodities, and its relative unimportance as a destination for agricultural exports. And further, if motor vehicle exports which account for about one third of country wide exports, all of which go to the American market, were removed from the Canadian numbers, the remaining spatial export markets would bear greater resemblance to the Western Canadian market.

The Japanese and Pacific Rim market represents on average only 8.5% of Canadian exports, the comparable figure for Western Canada is almost three times as great at 21.5%. If China is included within the Pacific Rim category, western exports rise to one quarter of national shipments. Countries in the region offer significant markets not only for grains but for a range of nonagricultural commodities including coal, metals, and forest products, but

Table 7.1: Geographic Markets: Percent Share for the Four Provinces, Western Canada, and Canada (1986-88 averages)

Spatial Market	Alberta	B.C.	Manitoba	Sask.	Western Canada	Canada
U. S.	71.55	44.97	57.07	39.74	54.06	75.30
Japan	6.54	26.30	7.63	10.63	15.93	5.78
Pacific Rim	4.68	7.19	2.36	4.64	5.59	2.72
W. Europe	2.59	13.40	10.45	6.23	8.50	8.33
Latin America	1.65	1.36	2.00	3.79	1.86	0.82
Central America	1.16	0.66	2.73	3.34	1.36	1.26
USSR,East Europe	2.87	0.20	6.16	10.75	3.13	1.07
China	2.94	1.61	5.87	11.41	3.82	1.36
Middle East	1.34	0.25	2.84	4.25	1.40	0.43
Africa	2.31	0.35	0.96	2.60	1.38	0.78
Other Asia	0.74	0.66	1.02	1.66	0.86	0.72
Australia, New Zealand	1.60	2.97	0.88	1.01	2.09	1.12
Total*	**100.0**	**100.0**	**100.0**	**100.0**	**100.0**	**100.0**

* Totals may not add to 100.0 because of rounding.

Source: Statistics Canada, *Exports by Country* (65-003).

there is also a strong desire in these markets to have as much as possible from the region in relatively unprocessed form. Effectively, the overwhelming proportion of national exports to the Pacific Rim are sourced in Western Canada and are made up of purchases of relatively unprocessed resources.

A second feature of the spatial profile is that markets in Eastern Europe (including the former USSR), the Middle East, and third world countries are of greater relative importance to western Canada. These shipments, largely but not entirely grains and also potash, are a primary basis of Canadian export relations with many of these countries.

Just as Western Canadian spatial markets show characteristics that distinguish them from the national, so there is notable variation across provinces. Based on aggregates, the province whose geographic pattern of exports, at least in the aggregate, most closely resembles the national in its dependence on the United States market is Alberta, with some 71% of shipments, largely energy or energy related items, going to that country. However, if the commodity composition of exports is considered together with their destination in the United States market, then Alberta is scarcely typical of the national situation. Japanese and Pacific Rim markets are somewhat more important to Alberta, and west European markets somewhat less significant, than for the country as a whole.

Both British Columbia and Saskatchewan stand in considerable contrast to Alberta. In the case of British Columbia some 45% of exports, largely forest products and metals, go to the United States, while some 35%, dominated by coal, forest products, and metals, go to Japan and other Pacific Rim countries. Western European shipments amount to more than 13% of exports with other spatial markets of minor significance. Though the proportion of Saskatchewan-sourced exports going to the United States market is around 40%, the figure is accounted for largely by potash, crude oil, and woodpulp. Japan and other Pacific Rim countries, including China, account for about one quarter of Saskatchewan exports. Another one fifth is found in Eastern Europe, the Middle East and third world countries. Some countries, such as Japan, South Korea, and a number in South East Asia, represent fairly stable markets for grain, but in the case of others such as China, and the former USSR, export sales constitute a residual supply to their domestic production and therefore may vary enormously from year to year.

Manitoba's proportion of exports to the United States market of 55-56% corresponds closely to the Western Canada figure. Yet if one excludes agricultural exports, approximately three quarters of nonagricultural exports, including commodities such as paperboard together with a variety of higher value added manufactured products, go to the United States market.

Summary

We have identified some dominant characteristics of Western Canadian and provincial trading relationships with the outside world. The importance of foreign trade is apparent in the proportion of exports to provincial GDPs. Employment in the primary industries both agricultural and nonagricultural, though a small share of total employment, is nevertheless significantly greater particularly in Alberta and Saskatchewan than in the country as a whole. The greater relative importance of employment in the primary sector is evident in a dominance of raw and fabricated materials in shipments. Further, exports tend to be highly concentrated, with some six commodities accounting for more than one half, and some fourteen making up two-thirds of the region's shipments abroad. In terms of spatial markets, export trade destinations for Canada as a whole are neither a good representation of flows originating in the region, nor in any of the four provinces, with Alberta perhaps an exception.

Commodity Price Volatility, Instability, and the Exchange Rate

2

This chapter will consider a number of questions important to Western Canada. The first evaluates the price behaviour of major commodity exports from the region. What kind of price cycles have been recorded in recent years? How volatile are they? Are they larger for some exports than for others? For the region's major exports, have price patterns in some differed from, or have they reinforced price patterns in others? How do the variances of price change in these commodities compare with variance in the inflation rate? The second set of questions addresses the economic stability of the region, with special reference to broad measures of activity. How do the four provinces compare with one another, with other provinces, and with the national average in terms of a generally accepted index of instability? The third set of questions concerns the exchange rate, a variable whose behaviour has stirred much controversy in Western Canada. It can be argued that depreciation in the external value of the currency can, through price effects, moderate, at least in some measure, the consequences for a region of unfavourable conditions in export markets, and of falling international levels of commodity prices. It is also clear that an appreciation in the external value of the currency can temper boom conditions in Western Canada when commodity prices are rising. Do presently available exchange rate indexes provide sufficient information to assess the impact of exchange rate changes on the region's economy? Did exchange rate behaviour serve to stabilize, or did it aggravate, economic conditions in Western Canada during the boom years of the seventies and the depressed period of the first half of the eighties? How do movements in the external value of the Canadian dollar compare to Western Canadian commodity price experiences? And what has been the effect of more recent trends in the external value of the Canadian dollar?

Commodity Price Movements

The volatility of the Western Canadian economy can be further understood against the background of price movements experienced by the region's major export commodity groups. For this purpose a Western Canadian commodity price index has been constructed for the period since 1972, containing both agricultural and nonagricultural commodities, and based almost entirely on United States dollar prices of the region's principal exports. The items contained in the index include wheat, barley, canola (rapeseed), softwood lumber, newsprint, woodpulp, natural gas, crude oil, coal, copper, zinc, nickel, aluminum, potash, salmon, and sulphur. The commodities and data sources are reported in Appendix C. The weight assigned each commodity is its value share in the average of the 1986 and 1987 exports from the region. The range of commodities includes not simply raw materials, but also processed items to which value has been added. The index is therefore neither exclusively a measure of raw material prices, nor is it a measure of the prices of processed materials. It is an estimate of prices, primarily in external markets, available to producers for primary products directly exported or for intermediate processed materials that taken together can be related to production planning in the region's key export industries.

The breadth of commodity coverage contained in the index suggests, not only wide variation in the channels through which marketing occurs, but also that the factors influencing specific commodity prices are diffuse. For example, commodity futures trading in highly developed markets occurs in agricultural products and metals, while in the case of forest products and energy these markets are, if not absent, then still quite limited. It is well known that fluctuations in agricultural prices are determined in large part by the influence of annual changes in production as well as on the willingness of market participants to hold existing commodity stocks. These annual changes represent year-to-year shocks on the potential supply occasioned by changing weather conditions, and by the effect of lagged price change on producer planting decisions. In effect, prices in these markets are strongly affected by supply shocks.

Market forces in the case of metals are different. Weather is unimportant and supply is responsive in the short run to market price variations. Because manufacturers, primarily durable manufacturers, are the basic users and because these industries are indeed sensitive to the business cycle, the role of demand is much more pronounced. In the case of copper about 40% of world consumption is accounted for by the United States, Japan, and West Germany, and their share of world consumption is comparable for the other base metals.

In the forest product industries, as in metals, supply can respond quite quickly to market conditions so that the role of residential construction, a dominant sectoral user of sawn lumber, is of primary importance in determining price. Woodpulp and newsprint prices reflect longer cycles in the growth of industry capacity, but also respond to demand conditions in the economy. In energy, throughout the period covered by the index, OPEC cartel actions to influence supply have been the significant influence on prices. For coal exports, prices are set by contract. In the case of sulphur and potash prices, they are also largely set by contract, though in the case of potash, spot sales are not unimportant.

To better report the price behaviour of commodities since the early seventies, Charts 2. 1(a) to (e) show the quarterly levels of the aggregate index, together with component indexes for each of four major groups: agriculture, forest products, energy, and metals. The aggregate index (1981 quarterly average=100) more than tripled between 1972 and 1981. The increase was far from steady with a post-1973 jump resulting from the combined impact of rising grain prices and the first OPEC price shock, and from a second jump in 1979 occasioned primarily by the second OPEC shock. The overall nominal index declined during the 1981-82 recession, recovered to 1981 levels in 1983 and 1984, and shows the general commodity market weakness from mid-1985 through the last quarter of 1986. From 1987 to 1989, the index rose and by the end of the latter year was substantially above the levels of the final quarter of 1986. The CPI measure of the domestic price level is also plotted in Chart 2. 1(e) for comparative purposes. It is apparent that prior to 1981 the real and not simply the nominal price of commodities in the aggregate increased. In contrast, since 1981 and throughout most of the decade the real price of Western Canadian commodities has fallen. The effects of the weakness of commodity price associated with the onset of the recession commencing in 1990 are quite apparent.

The figures also suggest that indexes for the major commodity groups show substantially different profiles over these years. Prior to 1981, the non-agricultural components of the index (including fish and potash not shown in the figures) showed sustained nominal increases, while agricultural prices displayed more variability reaching their highest levels in 1973 and 1974. The fact that nonagricultral commodity prices generally

Chart 1.2 (a) to (e): Western Commodity Price Indexes by Major Sector, and the Aggregate Index Compared to the CPI (1972/2 to 1990/4)

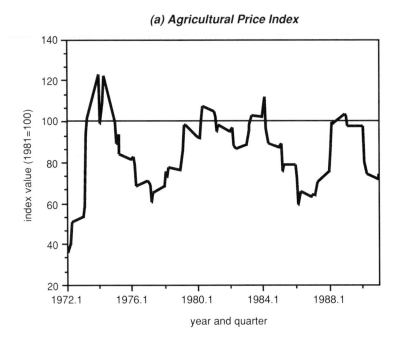

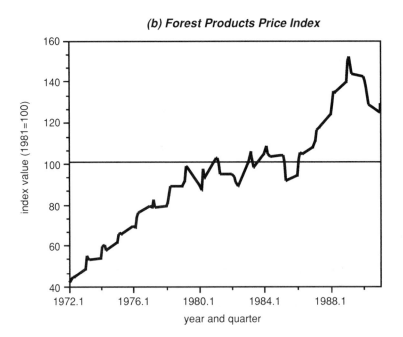

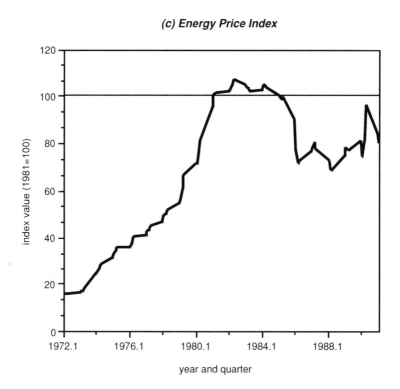

(c) Energy Price Index

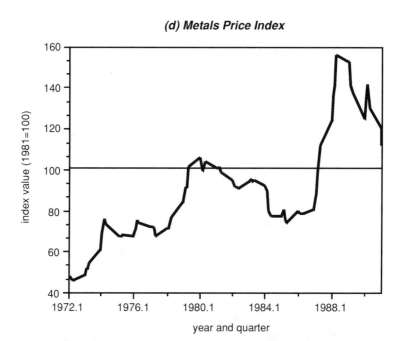

(d) Metals Price Index

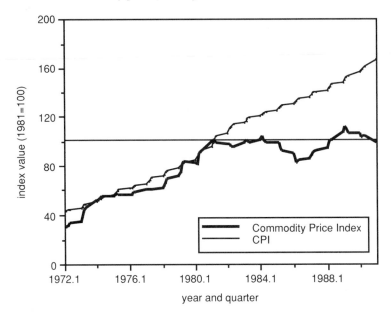

(e) Commodity Price Index and the CPI

moved in the same direction reinforced the economic boom in Western Canada during these years. In the 1981-85 period, agricultural prices continued their nominal variability while falling in real terms, metal prices fell in real and nominal terms, forest product prices moved within a narrow range nominally but fell in real terms, energy prices remained at high nominal levels but fell in real terms, potash prices fell sharply in real and nominal terms, fish real prices fell, and sulphur prices remained about constant in real terms. The condition of the energy industry was, of course, aggravated by the impacts of the National Energy Policy in the 1981-85 years. Certainly the behaviour of commodity prices in these years had a depressing overall effect on the economy of Western Canada in these years.

The behaviour of the components commencing in 1986 generally reflects the commodity price boom that preceded the onset of the North American recession. For example, from the beginning of 1986 through the final quarter of 1988 the forest index rose by 44%, and the metals index almost doubled over the same period. An exception was the energy index that showed little change in nominal terms from its lower 1986 levels. However, the agricultural index, potash, and fish prices also recovered sharply. With the increase in forest products, metals, and fish prices it is readily understandable why British Columbia experienced the most rapid growth of the four provinces in the post-1986 cyclical expansion.

Volatility in Commodity Prices

Prices in the markets for raw and semiprocessed materials are substantially more volatile than those in markets for finished goods. As products move through stages of production from raw materials, to processed commodities, to finished goods, they become more differentiated and lose their homogeneity. Effectively, nonprice product attributes emerge with added value, become more important at each stage of the production chain, and as this occurs the producer acquires a degree of market power. Further, as value is added incremental costs are incurred, many of contractual nature and distinctive product characteristics emerge, so that unit prices display less flexibility and greater stickiness. Since the region's exports are dominated by either raw materials or partially processed goods, it is instructive to consider the extent of price volatility for these products, and to compare it, for example, with that in other prices, in particular with flexibility in a widely accepted measure of the general price level such as the Consumer Price Index (CPI), or in the price of products at the factory gate as reported in the Industrial Products Price Index (IPPI).

Table 1.2 shows the standard deviation of quarterly price change for the four main Western Canadian export product groups over the period from the second quarter of 1972 to the second quarter of 1989. For comparative purposes the comparable coefficients for the CPI and the IPPI are also reported. Note that these coefficients are based on quarterly percentage rates of price change rather than on levels of prices, and therefore a direct comparison based on standard deviations is possible. The standard deviation for agricultural products substantially exceeds that for forest products, energy, and metals, but also for each commodity group the extent of price volatility over the entire period is very much larger than that in the CPI, ranging from a multiple of almost 12 in agriculture to approximately 5.3 in forest products. Comparable multiples for the IPPI are 7.9 in the case of agriculture and 3.5 in forest products.

While Table 1. 2 provides a summary statement of comparative variation over the entire period based on quarterly data, it is also useful to provide an alternative measure that informs about shorter term volatility. This is done by relating the annual standard deviation of the percentage price change for each group with a similar annual measure for the CPI, as in Chart 2. 2 (a) and (b). The comparison here is of the average squared deviation in monthly price change about the twelve month average for each year from 1972 to 1988. The results are reasonably consistent with those suggested by Table 1.2. Typically, the standard deviations calculated from the agricultural index are considerably more volatile than those estimated from other commodities but the volatility of price change in the latter, though less than in grain prices, still display substantially greater volatility than the CPI measure of inflation.

Table 1. 2: Standard Deviation of Quarterly Price Change for Main
Export Groups Compared with that in the CPI and the IPPI
(1972/2 to 1989/2)

Sector Price Index	Standard Deviation	Multiple of CPI Standard Deviation	Multiple of IPPI Standard Deviation
Agriculture	10.61	11.8	7.9
Forestry	4.78	5.3	3.5
Energy	5.4	6.3	4.0
Metals	5.14	6.0	3.9
Aggregate Primary Product Index (APPI)	3.56	4.0	2.6
Consumer Price Index (CPI)	0.90	–	26
Industrial Product Price Index (IPPI)	1.35	1.50	–

Source: Commodity price index coefficients and Aggregate Primary Product Index from price indexes constructed by the Western Centre for Economic Research; CPI coefficient calculated from Cansim D 484000; IPPI coefficient calculated from Cansim D 694000.

The obvious conclusion is that the prices of those exports that dominate Western Canada's trading relations with the international economy are extremely volatile by any standard of comparison.

The Terms of Trade

The well being of the residents of an area like the west is affected by the terms of international trade. The most commonly used measure of changes in them is the net barter terms of trade which is defined as the ratio of export to import prices. An improvement in the net barter terms of trade means that each unit of exports purchases more imports, while a decline means that more must be exported to purchase the same volume of imports as before. There is a strong positive relationship between movements in the terms of trade and real income in a region, at least in the short run, but the link is more tenuous in the longer term. An example is where productivity growth in the export sector leads to an increase in the volume of exports for a western product possessing some market power. The presence of market power means that the volume of the region's exports will influence the unit

Chart 2. 2 (a) and (b): Standard deviation of annual rates
of change in price indexes (1972 to 1988)

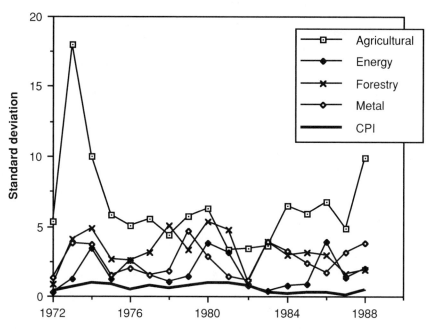

Graphs show standard deviation of monthly price change about the annual average

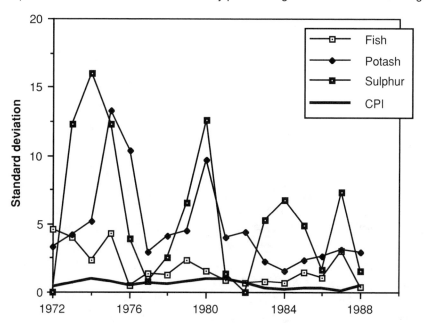

price of the commodity. The rise in exports will lead to a fall in unit price and hence a decline in the terms of trade. However, real incomes may still rise. The positive impact of productivity growth in the sector coupled with the economic resources freed up for use elsewhere may more than offset an adverse movement in the terms of trade.

Further, a sharp and sustained rise in the terms of trade may induce structural shifts within an economy that make it worse off in the longer term. Some oil exporting countries – Mexico, Nigeria, and Venezuela – suffered seriously because of sharply rising oil prices in the 1970s. Domestic inflation, especially rapid increases in service prices and/or rapidly appreciating currencies squeezed out traditional export industries and made it very difficult for import competing goods industries to survive. Even regional oil producing economies such as Texas and Alberta were subject to these forces but integration in a larger national economy significantly ameliorated the effects.

For Western Canada as a whole, the net barter terms of trade over the period 1972:1 to 1988:2 declined at an annual rate of 0.31%. In this calculation the export price is the Western Centre's aggregate products price index composed of a weighted average of the region's main exports, and import prices are represented by the IPPI, a proxy for the prices of manufactured goods. Chart 3.2 depicts the movements of the terms of trade for the period. The high degree of volatility of export prices discussed previously is evident. While the choice of time period in this calculation is important, the period chosen captures at least a full cycle in most resource price series.

Any discussion of movements in the terms of trade in Western Canada raises the question of whether fluctuations in commodity prices represent deviations about a trend,and are therefore expected to revert to the mean,or whether the commodity price change represents some permanent shift in the trend itself. The issues for a region are very different in the two cases. If the terms of trade always can be expected to revert to the mean the problem is one of stabilization rather than one of resource mobility and restructuring.

Measures of Regional and Provincial Instability

Mansell and Percy (1988) in the their recent study of the Alberta economy entitled *Strength in Adversity*, constructed indexes of provincial instability for a number of widely referred to economic measures such as employment, personal income, per capita personal income, output, and population. While there is no single, universally accepted method of measuring instability there are a number of widely used methods.

Chart 3.2: Western Canada Terms of Trade,
19972/1 to 1989/2 (1981=1.0)

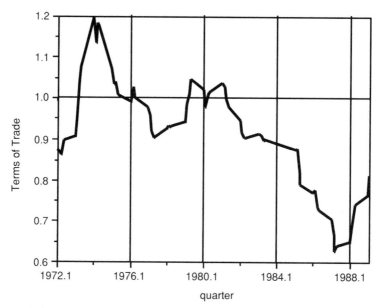

Source: Statistics Canada, *Industrial Products Price Index and Western Centre Index of Western Canadian Commodity Prices.*

Mansell and Percy adopted a portfolio variance approach favoured in the financial analysis literature. Applied to employment, for example, the portfolio approach uses measures of both variance and covariance to obtain an index of instability. The method sums each industry's variance (the squared differences of an industry's actual employment from its trend value) and its covariance (the extent to which these differences coincide with those in other industries). The square root of this sum is taken to obtain the basic number from which the index is derived. Specifically, if an industry has high employment variance, its employment fluctuates a great deal, and on occasion many workers in that industry will lose their jobs. A low covariance with a second industry in the province means that this industry may be expanding while the first contracts. In contrast, high covariance means not only that the two industries are laying off employees simultaneously, but also that under more favourable market circumstances they will be hiring simultaneously. When there is both high variance and covariance across industry employment, industries typically expand and contract together in a coupled, if not in a tightly linked, fashion. The results of this method applied to personal income payments by industry of origin at the provincial level are

Table 2.2: Indexes of Instability: Personal Income

	Index Level
Nova Scotia	124
New Brunswick	141
Ontario	159
Quebec	194
Newfoundland	194
Prince Edward Islan	215
Canada	216
Manitoba	254
Territories	336
British Columbia	533
Saskatchewan	720
Alberta	1328

Data cover the period 1961 - 1985.

Source: Percy, M. B. and R. L. Mansell, Strength in Adversity: A Study of the Alberta Economy, Table 4.1.

calculated and the results for each of the provinces and the national average shown in Table 2.2. Mansell and Percy point out that the values shown represent an ordinal rather than a cardinal measure of instability so that ,while the index for Ontario is 159 compared with that for Saskatchewan of 720, this does not mean that Saskatchewan's instability is 720/159 or 4.5 times that in Ontario. The measures do, however, reveal that Alberta, Saskatchewan, and British Columbia in that order have the highest indexes of personal income instability across provinces, while in contrast Manitoba's index is close to the national average. Similar instability rankings are found for other broad measures.

Volatility and the Domestic Economy

The high degree of volatility evident in personal income is also present in the individual components of aggregate demand. Most importantly, fixed capital formation is extremely volatile in Western Canada in comparison to other regions. Table 3.2 depicts a measure of its volatility by category for selected regions. In Western Canada both private and public fixed capital investments exhibit substantially greater volatility than in the rest of the Canada, with private fixed capital formation twice as volatile as elsewhere. The volatility in Alberta exceeds that of any other province for both public and private capital expenditure, while British Columbia ranks second.

Table 3.2: Standard Deviation of Annual Per Cent Changes in Real Fixed
Capital Investment, Selected Regions and Provinces (1972-1988)

Province/Region	Standard Deviation Private Sector	Standard Deviation Public Sector	Standard Deviation Sectors Combined
British Columbia	12.25	10.45	11.11
Alberta	14.17	16.29	13.41
Saskatchewan	11.51	9.23	10.45
Manitoba	10.23	8.74	9.04
Western Canada	10.66	8.88	9.65
Rest of Canada	5.33	5.96	4.90
Canada	6.25	4.10	5.44

Source: Statistics Canada, *Provincial Economic Accounts (13-213); National Income and Expenditure Accounts (13-001); Implicit Price Indexes in GDP (13-531).*

This high volatility of capital formation in the region derives from two sources. First, the amplitude of swings in export prices undoubtedly influences fixed capital spending. Large movements in export prices generate fluctuating returns to investment and in the export sector cash flow. Periods of rising export prices will be accompanied by investments as business attempts to add additional capacity. In contrast, during periods of falling prices firms will find themselves with declining profit margins and excess capacity. The response is to cut back on planned investments. Volatility is likely to be high because expectations play such a large role in decision making. The "boom and bust" cycle so evident in the west, particularly in the three western most provinces, comes in no small measure from the volatility of capital formation.

The second factor that increases the amplitude of swings in capital formation is the nature of labour force adjustments to cycles in economic activity. International and interprovincial migration play a significant role in meeting shifts in labour demand in the region. These swings in regional population also induce rises and falls in population-sensitive capital formation such as residential construction and public infrastructure.

Further evidence of the volatility of the Western Canadian economy is reflected in movements in land prices. Changes in land prices should provide a good measure of volatility as the value of land should capitalize expectations about future levels of economic activity. The demand for land comes ultimately from the level and pace of economic activity in the region. Hence, variability in an economy and the occurrence of unanticipated shocks

Table 4.2: Standard Deviation of the Annual Per Cent Change in Land Prices for Selected Cities Compared to the IPPI (1976-1987)

City	Standard Deviation
Canada: all city average	4.80
Toronto	4.57
Winnipeg	4.78
Regina	4.18
Edmonton	10.44
Vancouver	16.14
IPPI	3.80

Source: Statistics Canada, Construction Price Statistics (62-007); Industry Product Price Indexes (Cansim D 550000).

should also be reflected in land prices. Table 4.2 contains estimates of the volatility of land prices for selected cities. Both Vancouver and Edmonton exhibit a greater volatility than does Canada as a whole, or other cities. The low level of volatility in Winnipeg is not surprising given the relative stability of the Manitoba economy. That in Regina is more so, but the relative size of the public sector presence there is a tempering influence.

Effects of the Exchange Rate on Western Canada

No economic and financial indicator creates more controversy in Western Canada than the foreign exchange value of the Canadian dollar. (We define the exchange rate in the subsequent discussion as the value of foreign currency per unit of domestic currency, so that if we acquire less foreign currency per Canadian dollar there is a depreciation of the dollar, and if we can buy more foreign currency per Canadian dollar there is an appreciation of the dollar.) In the previous section the volatility of commodity prices has been considered and contrasted with volatility in generally accepted measures of inflation. In the post-1973 years, following adoption of a regime of floating exchange rates by the international economy, volatility in the external value of the currency has been added to the commodity price volatility facing western producers.

Variations in the external value of currency can, of course, be positive in their effects on Canadian producers if they serve to offset fluctuations in commodity prices. Thus, a reasonable generalization about Western Canada's major exports is that they are sold on world markets at prices determined in those markets. Perhaps in the case of sulphur, potash, and natural gas the volume of exports may have some influence on market prices, and though there is some product differentiation in other goods, such as wheat with its high protein content and rigorous grading standards, there nevertheless must be pretty strict adherence to international prices if market shares are to be retained. Because the exported products of Western Canadian producers are not easily differentiated in their attributes from those of international competitors, changes in the external value of the dollar directly affect company gross margins. Appreciation reduces the proceeds in Canadian dollars of sales occurring in those commodity markets where price is predetermined by market forces. The result is a reduced net margin. In a similar fashion, depreciation increases the proceeds in Canadian dollars of sales at these predetermined prices. Net effects on profitability may be somewhat less than gross effects since the latter, in limited degree, will be offset by whatever impacts appreciation or depreciation may have on producer unit costs. In sum, when commodity prices are falling, the adverse effects of the decline on the operating position of Western Canadian producers may be countered, in some degree, by a depreciation in the external value of the Canadian dollar, and when commodity prices are rising the boom effects of higher gross margins may be tempered by an appreciation.

Needless to say, exchange rate changes will have perverse effects on producers if appreciation accompanies commodity price declines and depreciation accompanies commodity price increases. It is therefore apparent why the level and the rate of change in the external value of the currency bring such expressions of concern in Western Canada.

It is also evident that, since the region competes internationally, the exchange rates of all major currencies, not just the United States dollar rate, matter to the Western Canadian economy. Though the United States is Canada's major trading partner and also the major trading partner of the four western provinces, yet it is far from the region's only trading partner, and certainly not its only foreign competitor. Measures indicative of the effects of exchange rate movements on Western Canadian export competitiveness are therefore required to interpret how changes in the external value of the currency have affected the region.

Exchange Rate Indexes

A comprehensive view of Canada's external currency position can only be provided by a trade weighted index, also referred to as an effective exchange rate. It provides a summary measure of the international value of a particular currency. There are a number of ways to go about constructing such an index, but they are always based on a weighted basket of currencies. To assess the effect of exchange rate developments on Western Canada we will use three such indexes: the Bank of Canada's G-10 effective exchange rate; the International Monetary Fund's (IMF) multilateral indexes of effective exchange rates; and a new index of effective exchange rates developed by the Western Centre that is specific to Western Canada and designed to measure the region's export competitiveness in world markets.

The Bank of Canada's G-10 Index. The Bank of Canada's G-10 index is weighted by Canada's direct trade with the 10 major industrialized countries: Belgium, France, West Germany, Italy, Japan, the Netherlands, Sweden, Switzerland, the United Kingdom, and the United States. Weights are shown in Appendix C. These countries account for nearly two-thirds of world trade and their importance in international financial flows is very much greater. Further, many countries not included in the group may link their own currencies to one or more of those in the index or use these currencies for their international transactions. Nevertheless, the fact remains that the G-10 index is based on bilateral rather than multilateral trade weights and is therefore an incomplete description of Canada's competitive position since the weighting system ignores the effects of head to head third market rivalry. For example, the G-10 index while it includes Sweden assigns to that country a weight based upon direct trade with Canada which is very small. However, Western Canada and Sweden actively compete in supplying third markets with wood and paper products. Neither does the G-10 index include Finland or Australia, two other countries with which Western Canada competes aggressively in third markets. It is possible to generalize by saying that weights in the G-10 index are related to success: the greater Canadian direct trade with a country the greater its weight in the index. But it may be in trade with those countries with a small weight that the exchange rate is crucially important.

The G-10 index for the period from 1975 to 1989 is shown in Chart 4. 2. The vertical axis is a measure of value of the Canadian dollar in terms of market basket of other currencies. If the graph is rising, the dollar is appreciating; if the graph is falling, the dollar is depreciating.

Two features need emphasis. The first is the marked decline in the index during the period from 1976 through 1979, and the second is the relative stability of the index from 1980 through late 1983 and early 1984. Effectively, the G-10 index shows in the late seventies a significant depreciation in the nominal value of the domestic currency during a period of nominal and real price increases in major Western Canadian export markets. This suggests that the exchange rate gave further impetus to the boom conditions prevailing in the region at the time. However, during the early eighties when

Chart 4.2: Bank of Canada G-10 Nominal Exchange Rate Index,
1975/1 to 1991/2

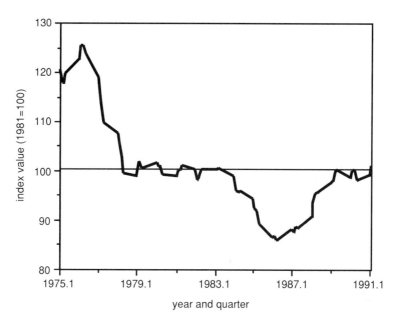

Source: *Bank of Canada Review*

Western Canada was suffering not only from the national business cycle but also from weakened nominal and falling real prices for its major export commodities, the G-10 nominal exchange rate index moved sideways suggesting that its time path did not in fact buffer the region against adverse international market conditions.

International Monetary Fund Exchange Rate Indexes. Two IMF indexes of effective exchange rates, one based on nominal and the other on real values, are a superior alternative for evaluating the effects of the exchange rate on Western Canada. These measures, using weights derived from the agency's multilateral exchange rate model, include third party competitive effects. The currency basket of the Bank of Canada G-10 index shown in Appendix C does not contain countries like Australia which vigorously compete with Western Canadian exporters though there is not a great deal of direct merchandise trade with that country. The introduction of third country effects into an exchange rate index can have a substantial impact on the currency market basket weights. For example, in the Bank's G-10 index, the United States has a weight of 0.8180 based entirely on bilateral trade flows, while Australia, not a G-10 country, is automatically excluded from the currency basket. But in the IMF indexes, the weight assigned the United States dollar is 0.6420 while Australia is included with a weight of 0.0370. Similarly, direct trade between Canada and Sweden is small with the Swedish weight in the G-10 index being 0.0050, while in the IMF indexes it is more than three times larger at 0.0164. The point is that estimates derived from a bilaterally based index will produce substantially different estimates from those based on a multilateral weighting system. The country weights contained in the IMF indexes are shown in Appendix D. The IMF publishes a number of real effective rate indexes, each the result of an alternative proxy for differential inflation rate adjustments. The version for Canada reported here is derived from the nominal index by applying to the latter a comparative inflation rate adjustment proxied by rates of change in "normalized" unit labour costs in manufacturing. The actual unit labour cost index is the product of two other indexes:

(a) output per unit of labour input (labour productivity), and

(b) the nominal wage rate.

Normal unit labour cost is actual labour cost adjusted for the impact of the business cycle on labour productivity. If differentials in unit labour cost inflation proxies are exactly reflected in movements in the nominal exchange rate index, then the real and nominal exchange rates coincide, and the country's competitive position remains unchanged. To the extent that changes in the nominal index do not correspond precisely with inflation rate differentials competitive positions are altered. For example, when the inflation rate for a given country exceeds the weighted average of inflation in the currency basket countries, and if this is not fully mirrored in a fall in the currency's external market value, then a real appreciation has occurred, and the country's competitive position deteriorates. In contrast, if the fall in the external value of the currency exceeds the inflation rate differential, then a real depreciation has occurred, and the country's competitive position has improved.

The two IMF indexes covering the period from 1975 through 1989 are in Chart 5. 2. The nominal index tells, in broad outline, a similar story to the G-10 index during the late seventies, though in the early eighties there is evidence of a nominal appreciation, with the index rising by approximately three percent between the latter part of 1980 and the last half of 1983. However, the index of real effective exchange rates clearly shows the adverse effects on Western Canada of the exchange rate path during the late seventies and early eighties. The index depreciates by some 25% between the third quarter of 1976 and mid-1980, and is followed by an appreciation of 16% through late 1983. The evidence from the IMF's real index is that the

Chart 5.2: Western Centre Nominal and Real Exchange
Rate Exchange Index, 1975:1-1988:4

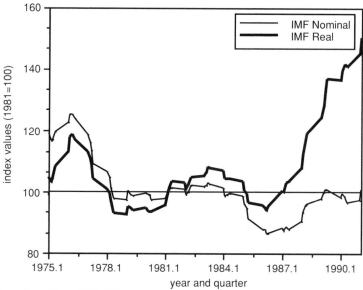

Source: *International Financial Statistics.*

exchange rate accentuated boom conditions in the West over the first period
when resource real prices were rising (by 9%), and when employment was
rising by 25%, compared with a rate of 12% in the rest of Canada. Exchange
rate appreciation worsened the region's difficulties in the period of the early
eighties, when resource real prices initially weakened, and then declined by
16% from mid-1981 through the fourth quarter of 1983. Employment in
Western Canada declined by 4% between mid-1981 and the fourth quarter of
1983. By that time, employment in the rest of Canada, though 1.4% lower
than its mid-1981 cyclical peak, had nevertheless recovered significantly
from its fourth quarter of 1982 cyclical low.

It is noted that since the first quarter of 1986, in contrast to the procyclical
effects of the earlier periods, the IMF real effective exchange rate appreciated
coinciding with increases in commodity prices and reflecting the positive
role for the exchange rate in disciplining their potential boom effects.
However, in the period since the beginning of the recession in the spring of
1990 the real rate has appreciated markedly thus intensifying cyclical
difficulties. It is noteworthy that no other industrialized country has
recorded anything approaching the rate of appreciation in the Canadian real
effective exchange rate (based on normalized unit labour costs) during this
period as reported by the IMF.

The Western Centre Exchange Rate Indexes. The final effective exchange rate indexes presented are specific to Western Canada in the sense that they are aimed at measuring the effect of exchange rates on the region's export competitiveness. We have constructed these measures because a national index can give misleading signals where the product composition of the region's foreign exports is clearly distinctive and where the relative importance of trading partners also differs from the national. The specific commodities included in the Western Centre index are crude oil, natural gas, copper, softwood lumber, woodpulp, newsprint, sulphur, coal, zinc, potash, wheat, canola, and barley. A double weighting system is applied in calculating the index, with the weight assigned a given country's currency in the basket derived from two components:

(a) an estimate of the given country's share in the total designated set of commodity imports of countries included in the currency basket (including home supplies to domestic markets); and

(b) Western Canada's export shares with respect to the same countries. Data limitations required the use of a fixed weighting scheme, and those estimated and applied were derived from trade data averages for 1986 and 1987.

This poses some difficulty and obviously makes interpretation of index behaviour in the earlier years tentative. Chart 6.2 shows the quarterly nominal and real effective exchange rate index measured by this method for the period from 1975 through 1990. The real index is obtained in this case by deflating the nominal index by the relative CPIs of Canada and countries in the currency basket. The index described in Appendix E takes account of third country effects with multilateral weights based upon two market share measures. The first is a set of ratios showing the distribution of the given product market in each country between domestic production in that country, and imports of that commodity from each of the other currency basket countries. For example, where the product is coal, the market shares for Japan represent the relative contributions of domestic production and imports from each of the other currency basket countries in satisfying Japanese requirements. A similar calculation is made for each commodity in each country. The second ratio applied to each commodity is the share of each currency basket country as a market for Western Canadian exports. This is essentially an export share ratio for each commodity. The set of country weights for the final index is calculated first, by applying to the country weights for each individual commodity the relative importance of that commodity in total Western Canadian exports, and then by summing across the results. In this index, the United States weight is .6209, the Australian

Chart 6.2: Western Centre Nominal and Real Effective Exchange Rate Indexes, 1975/1 to 1991/2

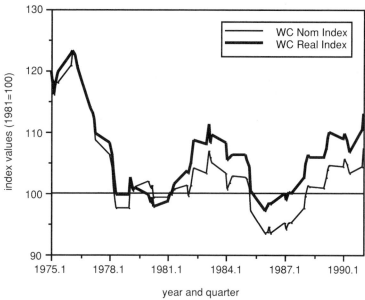

Source: See Appendix E.

.0955, and the Japanese .0830. The next highest weight is that for the United Kingdom at .0487. Chart 6.2 compared with Chart 5.2 shows that movements in the Western Centre index display a pattern quite similar to that in the IMF index, and thus leading to a simlar interpretation of exchange rate impacts.

Summary on the Exchange Rate

During the eighties the Bank of Canada's actions to resist depreciation against the American dollar, and therefore allow a general appreciation of the Canadian dollar against all currencies, was justified in pursuit of a lowered inflation rate and also, at least in some degree, to exert added pressure on business for actions to increase productivity. However, as the evidence here shows, this policy had severe consequences for Western Canada. It was procyclical in that it reinforced the effects of changes in commodity prices rather than offsetting them. If more appropriate measures of the exchange rate had been available during this period, the level of debate over exchange rate policy could well have been sharper, and the issues more readily identified.

The above evaluation of exchange rate movements since the mid-70s is not necessarily an argument that real devaluation in the external value of the currency is a necessary condition for remedying a region's economic difficulties. There is a prevailing view that devaluation is bad, that it emphasizes the costs of declines in the external value of the currency, worsens the terms of trade, and leaves the nation poorer because its exports have less buying power. Further, economists are in dispute as to whether inflation causes devaluation, or devaluation causes inflation. If depreciation causes inflation through

(a) raising the price of imports and domestically produced competitive goods,

(b) raising the domestic price of export commodities, and

(c) setting off inflationary expectations,

and if depreciation also takes pressure off the need to constrain unit production costs through productivity gains, then the external depreciation of the currency cannot be an effective instrument to restore competitiveness. The point is that when devaluation brings increases in domestic prices and wages, then any competitive gains are short term and quickly eroded.

The question remains as to whether this line of argument can be applied to Canada. We may note that in the wake of real appreciation of the Canadian dollar since early 1986, the trade balance deteriorated as might be expected, and in both 1989 and 1990 was quite low relative to the 1986-88 average. However, few could argue strongly that we enjoyed any perceptible improvement in productivity in response to exchange appreciation.

Does Canada have a defined, fully enunciated exchange rate policy? The answer is surely no. We can only conclude that when the monetary authorities elect to use, wisely or unwisely, the exchange rate as an intervening macroeconomic variable, their actions will be dictated by *ad hoc* objectives that are "national" in scope, not to offset the effects on Western Canada of changes in commodity prices and market opportunities.

Employment Effects of Commodity Prices and the Exchange Rate

There has been considerable stress in the above discussion on the combined effects of movements in exchange rates and in commodity prices on the Western Canadian economy. It has been pointed out that movements in the exchange rate may offset the effects of commodity price changes on producers: an appreciation moderating the effects of commodity price increases, and depreciation compensating for commodity price declines. However, if appreciation accompanies commodity price declines, and depreciation accompanies commodity price increase, the effect is

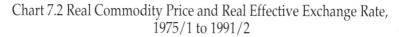

Chart 7.2 Real Commodity Price and Real Effective Exchange Rate, 1975/1 to 1991/2

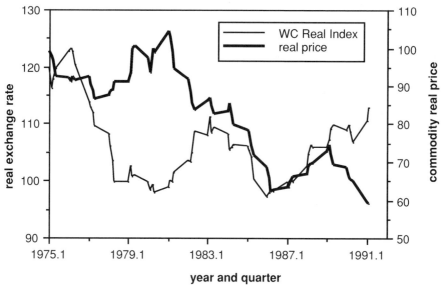

Source: See Appendices B and E.

destabilizing. Chart 7.2 plots the quarterly level of real commodity prices and the Western Centre's real effective exchange rate from 1975 to 1991. It is apparent that in the Western Canadian economic expansion and the ensuing recession that movements in the exchange rate had a pro-cyclical effect. On the other hand, from 1984 through 1989 movements in the real exchange rate compensated for real commodity price changes. Movements in the exchange rate again had a perverse effect in the 1990-91 recession.

It is important to provide a quantitative estimate of the effects of the real exchange rate and real commodity prices on the aggregate economy in Western Canada. We have applied a quarterly rate of change model to test for the effects of the real exchange rate and commodity prices on employment used as a proxy for the aggregate economy. The period is from the second quarter of 1976 to the second quarter of 1991. All variables are in percen tage rates of change. The dependent variable is the annualized percent change in monthly average employment per quarter, and the two independent variables are annualized percent changes in quarterly levels of

(a)   real commodity prices (the Western Centre commodity price index deflated by the national CPI), and

(b)   the Western Centre index of real effective exchange rates.

The results from the regression model support the important effect of these two variables on the Western Canadian economy. The estimate is that cumulative effect over three quarters of a rise of 1% in real commodity prices is a 0.2% increase in employment, while an increase in the real effective exchange rate of 1% leads to a 0.2% fall in employment. Taken together the impact of these two variables is considerable. The full regression model is reported in Appendix F.

3 Buffers and Strategic Options for the Private Sector

The Western Canadian reality in global markets is as an exporter of either raw or partially processed and therefore price sensitive commodities. Generally, with but few exceptions such as potash and sulphur, the region's export industries are in a price taker position. Their difficulties are compounded by developments over the past quarter century. The International Wheat Agreement which in earlier postwar years gave price and market stability has collapsed. The European Economic Community has emerged as a new and important player in the export market for wheat. Bio-technology, fertilizers and agricultural subsidies have radically altered the nature of the grain trade. The stability of oil prices is no longer guaranteed through the control of international markets by the seven major integrated petroleum giants, as in the early seventies, but now is largely dependent on the production decisions of the OPEC cartel. In the case of the copper industry, the spread of technology, the discovery of new deposits, and the nationalization of production facilities in LDCs have drastically changed the structure of the industry. Where Western Canadian companies are high cost producers in coking coal, compared with major competitors in Australia and South Africa, the outlook is not promising in the face of forecasts of relatively static demand by steel producers and of the ease with which other fuels can be substituted in production technologies. Conventional crude oil reserves are declining, costs of extraction are increasing, and, more generally, concerns over the adverse environmental impacts of fossil fuels are likely to accelerate the projected decline in the relative importance of oil as an energy source. Of course, in the case of natural gas, developments are more positive with market opportunities excellent for the environmentally clean fuel. On the other hand, the forest products industry has come under considerable market pressure from alternative sources of supply and will continue to operate under intense environmental scrutiny.

Institutional Buffers

Given the economic circumstances that have been sketched, a number of institutional buffers have been put in place providing partial insulation to particular producers from developments in specific international markets. These buffers are most evident in the agricultural and energy sectors. They have been discussed extensively elsewhere and it is appropriate here only to summarize the main features of selected programs and of the marketing agencies involved.

Selected Programs

Agriculture

In agriculture the buffer programs represent a combination of provincial and federal initiatives, some entirely publicly funded, and some funded jointly by producers and by government monies. They cover agricultural credit, transportation subsidies, crop insurance, and income stabilization for grain producers.

Agricultural Credit

Both the federal and the provincial governments are active farm lenders. There is considerable evidence that during the period of the seventies and early eighties these agencies, by increasing loan limits and by raising loan to market value ratios, added to volatility in the grain sector by (a) reinforcing the rise in farm land values and (b) by increasing the financial vulnerability of producers to any weakening in international grain prices.

In 1991 the federal government introduced a new program, the Gross Revenue Insurance Plan (GRIP), to be delivered through provincial crop insurance agencies and to integrate crop insurance with price support. Under this program grain and oilseed producers can sign up simultaneously for both yield and revenue protection with crop losses valued at an indexed 15-year moving average unit price.

Transportation Subsidies

Transport subsidies paid to grain producers are an important historical legacy. Most recently the Western Grain Transportation Act of 1983 replaced the historical, fixed Crow Rate on grain shipments to export terminals with direct annual payments of a freight subsidy to the railroads supplemented by additional payments if certain specified cost conditions are exceeded. Payment of the subsidy directly to the railroads has been heavily criticized on a variety of grounds including the following:

(a) it has a restrictive effect on adaptations in the transportation infrastructure;

(b) it raises grain prices in the prairie provinces by the amount of the subsidy and works against the expansion of the livestock industry feeding local grains to their cattle and hogs;

(c) and it is regarded by international grain competitors as an export subsidy because it supports shipments of specific commodities only.

Crop Insurance

These programs, which differ only slightly between Manitoba, Saskatchewan, and Alberta, are aimed at reducing fluctuations in the gross farm receipts of grain growers from natural hazards such as drought, frost, hail, insects, and the like. Coverage is up to 60 to 70% of the historical average yield for the risk areas based on farm location and soil class. Participation is optional, funding is from premiums paid by producers and matched by the federal government, and program administration is in the hands of the provinces.

Income Stabilization

The Western Grain Stabilization Act of 1976 set up a program for joint contributions by the federal government and by western grain and oilseed producers to an income stabilization fund. The program resembles an insurance scheme for farm cash flow. Producer participation is voluntary with levies now at 4% of sales, while the federal government contribution is 6%. The program's objective is to provide producers a floor in cash flow, ensuring that for any given year it will not fall below the average of the previous five years. In 1986 and subsequent years, the income stabilization program has been supplemented by the Special Canadian Grains Program that provides direct cash subsidies to grain producers to cushion the effects of weak international grain prices. Estimates are that federal and provincial government subsidies to grain producers in the four years from 1986 to 1989 ranged from just over $1 billion in 1986 to more than $2.4 billion in 1987 (Statistics Canada, *Canadian Economic Observer*, May 1991).

Energy

In the energy sector numerous fiscal programs have been introduced by both the federal and provincial governments in response to changing international oil prices. The assessment of the impact of the National Energy Program on the oil and gas industry and the Province of Alberta can be found elsewhere and will not be repeated here [Mansell and Percy, 1990, and Scarfe, 1985]. Provincial programs have generally buffered the industry through a variety of actions primarily of a tax expenditure character. These include adjusting royalty rates on existing wells to changes in international prices by providing credits against corporate income tax liabilities for royalties paid, by instituting royalty holidays for specified periods in the case of new oil and gas wells, and by cash grants in support of exploration and development work.

Marketing Agencies

Three marketing agencies play a significant role as intermediaries between producers and consumers in the export markets for Western Canadian commodities: the Canadian Wheat Board, Canpotex, and Cansulex.

Canadian Wheat Board (CWB)

CWB is a central marketing agency whose main purpose is to market overseas wheat and barley produced in Alberta, Manitoba, Saskatchewan, and the Peace River district of British Columbia All export sales of these grains occur through CWB which operates by both pooling and equalizing the returns to producers (subject to grade and farm location) from grain sales. The timing of grain deliveries from the farm, the route by which grain is exported, and the actual price paid by the overseas purchaser do not affect the returns to the individual producer. Under the pooling system, producers receive an initial payment on delivery that is based on price per metric ton established annually prior to spring planting. In fact this price becomes a floor price to producers for the coming crop year. Revenues received by CWB each market year (August to July) from the sale of grain are pooled and, where a surplus above initial payments and marketing costs occurs, it is distributed as a final payment to producers pro-rated by the volume of their deliveries. If annual sales returns are insufficient to cover the sum of initial payments and marketing costs, the deficit is covered by the federal government.

Canadian Potash Export Association (Canpotex)

Canpotex, with head office in Saskatoon, is a voluntary, privately owned and operated export consortium of Saskatchewan potash producers. While potash sales into the United States market are made by individual producers, off-shore sales are made through the Canpotex selling agency which enters into sales contracts and handles the transportation arrangements from the mines to the port of Vancouver. The fact that Canpotex is a voluntary association exposes it to the free rider problem, and since its formation in the seventies there have been few occasions when all producers have been members at any one time. The problem of adoption and pursuit of policies that realistically accommodate to the potentially divergent business strategies of the members is present in any voluntary organization. While observers judge that Canpotex has been reasonably successful as voluntary consortia go, it has also been pointed out that this may have largely been due to a combination of dominant market position, efficient producers, and a considerable degree of cohesiveness among them. The effectiveness of Canpotex could be increased by a requirement that potash producers be members of the association.

Canadian Sulphur Exporters Association (Cansulex)

This organization, with corporate offices in Vancouver, is a voluntary, privately owned export consortia of some 14 of the larger Alberta-based sulphur producers. The off-shore sales that are dominant are made through Cansulex. Offshore sales by Cansulex originate entirely in Alberta and account for about 40 to 45% of shipments through Vancouver. The balance of sales occurs through Shell and Amoco, which sell independently, and from Petrosul International. Petrosul is a competing marketing organization that, under an arrangement with the British Columbia government, buys sulphur production from the sour gas plants in that province. Though Western Canadian sulphur production is internationally cost efficient, export marketing remains fragmented despite the position of Cansulex. To a significant degree, fragmentation is the result of two distinct marketing approaches: price stabilization favored on the one hand by Cansulex and Shell, and volume or market share targets favored on the other hand by brokers and non-Cansulex independents. The obstacles to a single export marketing agency in the case of sulphur are divergent corporate strategies, as well as the fact that the Alberta government has been supportive of Cansulex, and the British Columbia government has designated Petrosul as a marketing agent.

Strategic Options: A Product/Market Approach

A realistic assessment of Western Canada's export based economy points to potential longer term vulnerability despite the many advantages possessed by the region. It is a producer of relatively undifferentiated commodities sold by mature industries primarily on a price basis . The region is fortunate to possess a wide range of raw materials; in the extraction of some it is a low cost, efficient producer, but in others it is a high cost producer—albeit a reliable supplier because of its complex, capital intensive infrastructure—and its position fragile. And in many of these materials new, lower cost producers have eroded or threaten to erode Western Canada's market share. As a region whose residents enjoy high living standards, one linked to the global economy through low value added, price sensitive commodities, it is absolutely critical that business and government think strategically about future evolution in the export base, as technology and industrial restructuring throughout the industrialized world transform international market and product opportunities. Beyond these concerns are effects the environmental movement exerts, and will continue to exert on Western Canada, including, for example, possible new legislation affecting the energy industry through taxes on carbon fuels, and affecting the forest products industry through mandates that printed materials use specified percentages of recycled newsprint.

The model in Figure 1.3 can be applied to the prevailing product/market position of Western Canadian producers. Though the model is generally used to illustrate the strategic options facing an individual enterprise, we adopt it here to better interpret prospects in the West.

To reiterate, the region's current export trade follows from comparative advantage, whether rooted in factor endowments, or in cost advantages generated over time by the dynamics of learning in the myriad decisions of business firms, large and small, old and new. The uppermost left-hand cell containing the region's exports represents the status quo with a narrow product base consisting largely of undifferentiated commodities. Markets, though somewhat less concentrated than for Canadian exports as a whole, still cannot be described as highly diversified. The status quo consists of the crude oil, natural gas, woodpulp, sawn lumber, grains, oilseeds, ore concentrates, potash and primary metals that connect western Canada to the world community. Exporting more of what the west now exports – selling raw materials into established markets – simply increases the dominance of price sensitive, resource commodities in this cell. Vertical downward movements from this cell alter the status quo by opening extended and/or new market opportunities for established products. Extended markets differ in degree from new markets. Extended markets might be expanded regional

Figure 1.3: A Product/Market Matrix

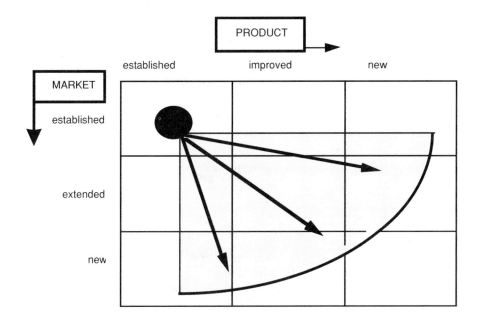

markets in the U.S. for natural gas made possible by the greater access available to energy producers under the FTA. In this case we have the greater exploitation of regional markets within a national market. An example of a totally new market for established products is the shipment of red meat to Pacific Rim countries made possible by more suitable channels of distribution and sales practices that are better tuned to customer needs.

In contrast, horizontal movements from the status quo occur either because of product modification or new product development. A transition to the horizontally adjacent cell implies more value added prior to export of resource based commodities. A further horizontal movement to the uppermost right hand cell implies the development of competitive advantage in a new range of products with relatively high value added content.

In a world driven by science and technology, maintaining competitive position in the 'established' product/'established' market cell is no easy task. Relative wage rates change, exchange rates are volatile, market preferences shift, and technology erodes the industrial uses of some resource commodities while creating new applications for others. Even if Western Canadian organizations were extremely vigilant in responding to these changes there is neither a guarantee that competitive advantage can be maintained, nor that our resource industries will be insulated from the effects of technology in altering the product preferences of consumers. It is clear that the long term health of the region requires transformation of the export base by searching for and realizing competitive advantage in other cells of the matrix. These efforts will focus on market and/or product changes. Whatever evolution occurs will be a joint outcome resulting from actions by businesses now located in the region, of decisions by firms to initiate operations in the west, and by the startups of indigenous entrepreneurs. In the next several paragraphs we consider briefly selected strategic options open to Western Canadian producers in maintaining present competitive advantage, or in finding new advantage through product and/or market adaptations.

Cost Leadership/Production Capabilities

The viable option for industries located in the established products/ established markets cell, producing standardized or undifferentiated products, is a competitive strategy that assigns the highest priority to cost leadership through state of the art production methods. The focus is on production capability, defined to include production know-how, processes, systems, and equipment required for extracting raw materials, and the capacity to improve those processes. Production capability underpins cost leadership. To be absolutely clear, cost leadership has positive not negative connotations. It does not mean that commodity producers seek to increase competitive advantage through cutting wages, for this action simply lowers living standards in the area. Lower wages mean reduced purchasing power for employees and, in consequence, lower income for the region. The central requirement to sustain living standards is state of the art production capability and steady improvements therein. Where relatively undifferentiated products are produced for export, competitive advantage is acquired and maintained by ever more efficient production methods, reinforced by an infrastructure with modern transportation and communications networks. Process innovation is the strategy for private sector producers coupled with a public policy commitment to a high quality, well-maintained infrastructure.

The focus on state of the art production methods, rather than on developing new products or markets, is one that progressive western producers have long opted for, and it is one with which they are quite comfortable. Innovative action of this type can be absorbed into operations either by improved managerial practices including the upgrading of labour, through improvements at the margin in existing techniques, or through capital outlays for machinery and equipment incorporating the newest technology as rapidly as possible. With mature products, and under the threat of enhanced supply from low wage offshore producers, the strategy of process innovation to enhance production capability is more compelling than ever. It will require that commodity producers in above normal years plough back above average earnings into capital equipment and employee training. The emphasis must be on cutting, digging, and reaping more efficiently. The argument is made even stronger by the fact that many of our most accessible forest and energy reserves have already been fully exploited, and unit costs of extraction are therefore under continuous upward pressure.

By employing increased production capability/cost effectiveness as the competitive strategy that is directed at maintaining an export base status quo, it is virtually certain that establishments in the region will adopt more capital intensive operations. While this strategy may not reduce the relative share of aggregate income originating in these activities, it will reduce the share – and probably the absolute numbers – employed in Western Canada's traditional export industries, and will require personnel with more technical training and higher skill levels i.e. with more advanced levels of numeracy and literacy.

The risk element in a strategy of cost leadership/enhanced production capability is acceptable to large, resource based business in Western Canada. Top management, for example, understands the risk involved in exploration and extraction of resources: it is clear what is being sought, when a discovery occurs, and how estimated returns on capital outlays can be calculated by standard methods. Risk calculations are easily made when a key assumption is that the world will remain pretty much as it is now, and therefore we will continue to do more of the same and do it more efficiently. However, there is peril in discounting too heavily the probabilities that status quo activities will be battered by a potent combination of the environmental movement, the thrust for sustainable economic development, restructuring, accelerated technical change, and the aspirations of newly industrializing countries (NICs) and LDCs. These forces cut across social, political, and economic change. They exacerbate price volatility in the commodity producing sector and magnify the effects of exposures to rapid and discontinuous external shocks. To dismiss these forces is even more dangerous when the region's exports are so highly specialized in a few relatively unprocessed commodities. These concerns cannot be avoided at the the level of the individual business. It has been argued recently that established firms in mature markets are vulnerable simply because extreme rationalization of technologies, work forces, and work processes introduces rigidities that erode flexibility in adapting to externally imposed change (Dertouzos, Lester and Solow, 1989). The question is whether a narrowly skilled organization will possess the resources to manage change successfully.

Finally, it should be pointed out that pursuit of a cost leadership/enhanced production capability strategy has in the recent past, and may very well in the future, invoke charges of unfair competition, subsidies, and other discriminatory threats from American interests, at least until some accommodation is struck respecting subsidies under GATT, or failing that, under the Free Trade Agreement. We will consider this further in Chapter 4.

Searching for Extended Product/Market Options in the Private Sector

In considering options that would enable the region's export base to move from the *status quo* , perhaps the single most important point is that it makes no sense for the region to abandon those activities in which it now enjoys significant competitive advantage internationally. The key background elements in the situational analysis of the West are:

1. a skilled satellite labour force with highly specialized groupings around energy, forest products, metals, and agriculture industries, and with educational attainment exceeding the Canadian average;

2. a systematized, well-maintained infrastructure encompassing a wide range of activities oriented to international trade;

3. a much expanded middle and upper class of entrepreneurs, professionals, and provincial and local government civil servants as compared with a generation ago;

4. natural resources, still in many instances of above average quality, but with a reserve adequacy for both nonrenewable and renewable resources considerably less than in earlier eras.

The problem is how, given this foundation, western activities can be leveraged into additional value added, an absolutely basic requirement for altering the *status quo*.

Export Sales of Professional Services

Any consideration of the export of professional services begins with the fact that they are embodied in the commodity exports of the region [Grubel and Walker 1989]. Professional service inputs are a necessary condition for low cost, high productivity producers. Further, high quality transportation services – rail, truck, pipeline, and air – are essential requirements for the efficient movement of commodities to market. The existing competitive advantage of the region is attributable to the fact that forest products, energy, and agricultural producers enjoy a degree of world leadership in production technology. Therefore industrial activities should be seen not simply in terms of a specific product set, such as sawn lumber, natural gas, or wheat but more broadly to include backward and forward linkages to professional servicing occupations. Included under this broader umbrella would be business and professional human services, such as foresters, geologists, engineers, agronomists, and computer software developers whose inputs are embodied in the outputs of resource based industries. Some of these professional services are imported from elsewhere in Canada or abroad, but many are headquartered in Western Canada, and well positioned to provide a range of consulting advice anywhere in the world. Studies of their activities during and subsequent to the depressed 1982-85 period in the west have verified the export capability of these professional service firms [Mansell and Percy 1990].

Services, unlike goods, are nonstorable, and since they are used as produced, interaction of a continuous nature between the user and the provider of the service is generally necessary, a circumstance which explains the present stock of professional service capacities domiciled in Western Canada. A transition from the status quo cell of Figure 1.3 to other cells can come through larger quantities of services embodied in exports. Value is added through the application of more services. This question as it relates to specific industry groups is taken up more fully later in this chapter.

When the potential for expanded service exports are considered, it is frequently their direct rather than embodied form. National governments apply widespread regulations and administrative procedures to the service provider generally under the rationale of protecting the service user. These rules are not presently harmonized under GATT. The export of services as an instrument of diversification therefore opens up the question of how providers are to be linked with their export clients. Given the presence of regulations, and the ease with which nontariff barriers can be applied, the export of professional services will almost always require an establishment on-site through which the services can be provided. Professional service exports will then have a dissimilar impact on the region of origin from that occasioned by their embodiment in goods' shipments. However, all factors considered, if more professional and technical services are embodied in the west's competitively based exports, i.e., add value to them, there is every reason to expect that the development of additional and complementary export capabilities in these highly skilled and specialized occupations is possible, indeed probable, and that headquarters should remain in Western Canada. More value added in our traditional export products should strengthen the potential for direct service exports.

There is for the record another side to the export of services. When expertise is made available to foreign producers, say in NICs or LDCs, the purpose is to transfer the most modern technology. The very transfer and application by producers in these areas can be instrumental in erasing advantages in cost and production capability presently enjoyed by Western Canadian raw material producers. This is but one more reason why the West would be unwise to assume that the future will neatly replicate the past.

Strategies for Changing the Export Base Status Quo

If the region is to diversify its present export base, it will result from a multitude of decisions taken inside individual business enterprises. Governments cannot alter economic structures; they cannot restructure economies in a society where allocation decisions are market determined. Yet it was not very comforting to read that recently the Chairman of Connaught BioSciences summarized the attitude of Canadian investors and senior management as follows:

> "If they can't dig it out of the ground, pump it out of the ground, or throw up a building they are not interested" (*Financial Post* September 1, 1989).

If this is an accurate representation of managerial judgment, then it poses a serious barrier to transitions from the export base status quo. Doing more of the same to the exclusion of alternatives is scarcely a strategy that regional business can adopt. The quotation, applied to companies producing raw or partially processed materials for export, conveys a mindset in which organizations are compelled to think volume, to do more of the same, to judge success in terms of selling as large a quantity of product as possible given the prevailing price, to focus on enhanced production efficiency and economies of scale. However, Western Canada, indeed the country as a whole, needs a more balanced combination of exports incorporating both new markets and new products. Existing approaches emphasizing more volume have to evolve a focus on better understanding customer needs and creating value to satisfy them.

We emphasize export diversification (not diversification for its own sake) in an internationally competitive framework as the only foundation with a realistic promise of permanence. What are the strategic considerations in moving to a larger proportion of export activities in the other cells of the matrix? What are the transformations necessary to secure this? What will be required to secure those changes? In all likelihood changes will necessitate much orderly, methodical effort – more research and development, new combinations of technology, marketing capacity, product quality, and labour skills. These transformations will not be easy, particularly when the perception of the upper-left-hand cell in Figure 1.3 is not one of established products and markets but rather is a current products/current markets mix. But new global realities offer no guarantee of the status quo. Quite the contrary.

It is unlikely that export diversification of any magnitude can be secured without a commitment by the region's larger enterprises. Two important matters are the degree to which these companies identify with the needs of the region and how their analyses of conditions are affected by corporate attitudes, particularly the attitudes of senior management. Are they receptive to making a serious exploration of what is required for such a transition? How may corporate structures have to change to introduce "intrapreneurial" leadership in the drive for new markets and/or new product options? Is management's horizon short term or long term with respect to economic returns? Examining options will require that the firm identify the capabilities that must be acquired, the new technologies and new human resources, for passage into the other cells of the matrix. How will these new requirements differ from in-house capabilities in terms of the knowledge and general training/education of technical managers in the organization? In a transition is the emphasis to be on new products and services, or is it be on new customer groups? Effectively, if change is to be secured, how are the boundary conditions for securing it to be rationalized? How much capital investment and how much personnel retraining may be required for an acceptable level of performance in the new activity? Within these organizations, strategic thinking will centre on choosing the primary thrusts of business development, on setting the priorities for products and markets, on involving an exploration of the new and unfamiliar. This exploration may expose the traditional resource based firm, not to well-understood production and exploration risks, but rather to forms of risk associated with the marketplace behaviour of competitors and buyers. Management will be concerned with how it can define the objectives and scope of a new market/new product thrust for risk assessment, with how it can identify major concrete steps as opposed to those necessary steps about which there is great deal more uncertainty. Defining strategic options as a central part of the search for possible new areas of competitive advantage is indeed a complex matter, yet to turn away simply because it is complex can leave cost leaders who continue a single minded pursuit of cost leadership ever more exposed.

A second important matter is the commitment of large organizations to research and development expenditures, including market research, since these expenditures appear to be necessary – if not a sufficient condition – for securing the needed transformations. The record here is not encouraging, for the fact is that industry in Canada, and Western Canada is no exception, does far less research as a proportion of output and sales than does industry in most other well developed nations. Indeed it has been estimated that even adjusting for the significance of the resource sectors in the Canadian economy, if the private sector in Canada did as much research as undertaken by the private sector on average in G-7 countries, research and development expenditures in the sector would have been 1.5% rather than 0.7% of output [Holbrook, 1989].

A recent study [Roussel, Saad and Erickson, 1991] identifies other problems in securing adequate returns from research and development expenditure. The authors conclude that firms may fail to get the full benefits because this activity is isolated from the rest of the organization not simply in a physical sense but, more importantly, in a cultural manner. They find that managers of production, marketing, and sales interact only infrequently with those in research and development. The result is that research and development goals tend to be biased toward technology rather than to the needs of the firm's customers. The authors suggest that research and development budgets be allocated on the basis of commercial as well as technological goals, and that internal research and development departments should compete with outside contractors as a means of subjecting research proposals to "peer review." This they regard as a means of reassuring both those engaged in the research as well as general managers.

New, small manufacturing enterprises also have their place in moving a larger share of a region's exports from the northwest into other cells [Schragge: 1985, Cameron 1984: and Lee, Tinga and Fortune 1988]. The choice of location by small enterprises appears to be determined more strongly by the personal preferences of the entrepreneur rather than by any innate comparative advantage that a particular area may have. This suggests that given the right combination of circumstances, one in which mechanisms exist for facilitating the complicated process of technology transfer between industry and university, spin-off small businesses can play a role in transitions to alternative product/market cells through product development. That is already evident in the emergence of bio-technology companies in the West.

A Public Sector Role?

We are clear that a transformation of the region's export base can occur only as a result of decisions taken within the business sector by large, medium, and smaller sized enterprises. What is the role of the federal and provincial governments in bringing about this change? The most important contribution that the public sector can make is in creating a supportive climate, one facilitating change. In a supportive climate, government

- provides information that contributes to the development of both new markets and new products;

- takes actions to encourage western exporters to add value to their products and thereby take maximum possible advantage of full tariff elimination under the FTA;

- recognizes that a labour force of the highest quality is a necessary condition for attaining desired transformations and that such a labour force is the product of a first class educational system;

- recognizes that publicly funded research and development and market research, are essential to breaking the established product/market cycles, and that a large share of this must be carried on in the region's universities;

- accepts that effective transfer to the private sector of technology generated by research and development and market research activities requires a collaborative structure in which industry is involved on an ongoing basis from the beginning;

- contributes to a stable economic environment through the pursuit of policies to smooth, insofar as possible, cycles in economic activity brought about by market forces;

- insures that the tax system does not discriminate against investments in unstable regional economies.

In regard to the last point, Mintz (1988, 226) has found that effective corporate tax rates for startup or new investments in Canada in the period 1979-81 were "...quite striking." Startup investments, which imply highly risky future returns, are especially penalized in the current tax system since fast write-offs and deductions cannot be used.

A number of the above actions are directed at the use of government fiscal policies to reduce risk. Many of the others stress the facilitating role of government in transferring knowledge into the export base. A necessary condition for a stronger value added orientation in this base is greatly strengthened research and development outlays. Although process innovation is unlikely to be reflected adequately in aggregate estimates of research and development outlays, the information contained in the recent OECD study *Innovation Policy:Western Provinces of Canada* (1988) is of concern. The monograph reports research and development expenditures and relates them to provincial GDPs. The figures for the year 1985 show that expenditures were 0.9% of provincial GDP in British Columbia, Alberta, and Saskatchewan and 1.1% in Manitoba. These figures are all below the Ontario figure of 1.7% and the national average of 1.4%, the lowest of the G-7 countries. In addition, research and development spending by industry accounted for a substantially lower proportion (from 10.8% in Manitoba to 34.4% in British Columbia) than in the country as a whole (47.9%). This is particularly disturbing (again notwithstanding the argument that Canada benefits from research and development done outside the country by multinationals operating in Canada), since a major and generally acknowledged criticism of the country's science and technology expenditure allocation is that an insufficient proportion is carried on by industry, where research results have commercial accountability through market driven product applications.

Examples of Transition Potential from the Forest Products Sector

The forest products sector accounts for between one-fifth and one-quarter of the region's merchandise exports with the overwhelming share sourced in British Columbia. Yet it is noteworthy that more than 90% were in low value added products. The output of the industry is dominated by construction lumber, market grade kraft pulp, and standard grade newsprint *[1984 Forest and Range Resource Analysis]*.

Some spatial diversification both in sawn lumber and woodpulp has taken place in the past two decades, in particular with the emergence of the Asian market. This is a positive development since their economic cycles are not highly synchronized with those in North America, but product adjustments are required. In sawn lumber, the housing architecture of Japan and other Asian countries requires that lumber be cut in sizes that differ from the North American and European markets. This effectively requires a change in work procedures from the timber tract to the point of embarkation [Stoffman, *Globe and Mail*, November 1990].

However, there is general agreement that further expansion in the forest industry in British Columbia will result only from getting more value out of increasingly costly raw materials [cf. *1984 Forest and Range Resource Analysis*]. Increased wood costs have eroded the competitiveness of the coastal industry, and expansion in the interior industry (which has meant an economical source of wood chips for pulp mills) can no longer continue. The problem of higher unit costs for softwood sawlogs is compounded by environmental concerns unfavourably affecting an industry built on access to live trees, and ranging all the way from resistance to clear cutting to newsprint recycling laws,

The move to exportable higher value added products in the lumber industry requires some restructuring, and it appears more attainable in the coastal industry where specialty products are produced even though sales are now oriented toward the domestic rather than the export market. In contrast, the almost exclusive focus of the interior mills is on producing a high volume of standardized products [*1984 Forest and Range Resource Analysis*]. Maintaining and expanding the value added market in forest products is an excellent example of the need to combine engineering and market research. Higher value added wood products, including ladders, furniture, mouldings, tool handles, railway ties, soffits, gutters, windows, doors, and others, are severely threatened by substitution from metals, plastics, concrete, or new ceramic materials. Research resulting in new technologies can limit wood substitution. Examples that have been given include fire retardant treatments, precision kiln drying to stabilize size, surface preservation and enhancement, adhesive technology, and densification. Yet despite the critical importance of research and development, recent estimates by the Dean of Forestry at the University of British Columbia are far from reassuring. It is estimated that the provincial industry spends 0.26% of gross forest sector sales on research and development while the comparable figures for the Swedish and U.S. industries are 1.7% and 1.5% respectively [*Globe and Mail*, September 26, 1990].

Adding value means transforming the material in a way that contributes to customer satisfaction; the necessary condition is combining market research with engineering-based research. It has been pointed out that the forest products industry lacks good information about how its products are actually used after they leave the factory gate. Once these flows are identified, the industry will be in a position to focus its research, development and product, promotion strategies. But again the market research record of the industry is poor. Recent estimates are that the sector spends only 0.2% of sales value on product promotion [*Federal Resource Development Report 068*, 1989].

Examples of Transition Potential from the Agricultural Sector

The grain sector offers at a basic level other specific examples of how market and scientific research might be combined to bring about transitions from the existing markets/products cell. It has been pointed out that, while grain markets in the industrialized countries are largely static, there is growing market potential in the developing world. [Gilson, 1989; and Veeman and Veeman, 1985]. The potential is apparent in predictions that in the next twenty years 950 of every 1000 births will occur in the developing countries. Yet though knowledge of demand potential for classes of grains in these countries is limited, what is known suggests that the export opportunities are most apparent in lower quality bread wheats, and more generally possible in those types of wheat not traditionally grown in Western Canada—such as 3M, hard red winter, utility, and soft white wheat varieties. Veeman and Veeman point out that recognition of these customer needs would enable grain producers to capitalize on both yield advantages and emerging opportunities in world trade. The more precise tailoring of grain production to market potential is not costless. It requires not only a prowess in market research but also agricultural research and development expenditures into higher-yielding strains of wheat and barley, and an agronomic and economic assessment of the feasibility of subregional specialization to accommodate these market opportunities. Recently, new evidence has been offered indicating that the benefits of a more market based orientation would be far from trivial [Ulrich, Furtan, and Schmitz, 1987]. The authors estimate that net economic returns to grain farmers would be 15 to 25% higher annually, and research into new grain technologies would be highly productive if the cultivation of medium and soft wheats were encouraged.

A recent development, still in its very early stages, is evidence of interest by the prairie pools in moving their activities downstream into food processing. Whether this strategy of adding value will prove effective remains to be seen. However, it is clear that whatever success occurs will depend in very large measure on the identification of customer tastes and preferences. Knowledge of final consumer wants, the capacity to create products that meet those wants, and the presence of a marketing and distribution system will all be essential.

Perhaps although not entirely appropriate to this section, readers will permit us to give an example of how customer access has been incorporated into selling strategy by the Saskatchewan potash industry. Potash producers have strengthened their international market position by working with customers to determine optimal fertilizer combinations of potash. The strategy of a strong customer orientation has been first to send technicians with the potash to demonstrate how it can be best applied at the farm level.

Secondly, agriculturalists from foreign countries have been sponsored into research programs at the University of Saskatchewan. Here is an example of an industry producing what would generally be described as an undifferentiated product but taking active steps to differentiate it by attaching service attributes of direct benefit to customers.

The livestock industry provides other examples of supplying a product suited only to tastes defined by the Canadian grading system [Kerr, 1985]. There is a rapidly expanding market for meat products which have high income elasticities of demand in Japan and other Pacific Rim countries. In the case of very limited Canadian sales of beef to Japan, a major impediment to increasing sales to that country is that Canadian beef is too lean for Japanese tastes. Kerr attributes the failure of Canadian producers to penetrate other Pacific Rim markets to price but suggests that it may be possible to compete, particularly with Australian producers, by adopting some form of grass-fed rather than grain-fed production technology. Research and development into feasible grass-fed technologies as well as market research into customer tastes are required. It has further been pointed out that industry to industry contacts between Western Canadian livestock producers and the beef-deficit California market have been very limited. The Free Trade Agreement in situations like this offers a substantial incentive to move old products into new markets.

Examples of Transition Potential from the Energy Sector

In the past generation, the petrochemical industry evolved as an important industrial sector in the west, particularly in Alberta. The industry, relying almost exclusively on natural gas feedstocks, is a major producer of commodity grade plastics including polyethylene, polyvinylchloride, and polystyrene. It is estimated that the polyethylene capacity in Alberta is sufficient to meet all demand in the western North American market.

Recent World Bank research points out that for developing countries a basic petrochemical industry has taken the place in economic growth plans once occupied by the iron and steel industry [*Technical Paper No. 84*, 1989]. The study indicates that in many applications commodity plastics face maturity, and it emphasizes that in highly developed countries industry movement further downstream to the production of high performance, high value added engineering plastics emerge as the most appropriate option. The demand for these downstream plastics in large degree results from the replacement of metals in the construction trade, of components and body parts in vehicles, of components in electronic hardware and appliances, and as adhesive materials. Growth in demand is estimated at rates of 10% or more annually, an amount measurably greater than projected demand for commodity grade plastics.

A natural evolution in the western industry is downstream into these materials. These products have a very high value to weight ratio, and there does not appear to be evidence of significant economies of scale in production. On the other hand, a necessary condition for success is a large research establishment in which customer needs are intimately linked to engineering and product development. Yet again, here is an option for broadening the region's economic base that is rooted in existing competitive advantage and its existing stock of industry expertise.

Conclusion

In the short term, Western Canada will continue to concentrate on what it does now—but it will have to do it better. In the intermediate term, it seems inevitable that if the region is not only to reduce volatility but also to sustain the relatively high levels of income it has enjoyed in the past, then value must be added in product areas where it possesses competitive strength. This will require a matrix of collaboration between government and business, between labour and management, between supplier performance and customer requirements, and between research in advanced educational institutions and its application in the development of marketable products by business enterprises. We do not believe that the government can pick winners in pursuit of higher value added, but we do believe it essential for government to support and maintain first class educational institutions that provide to the region a well-trained, flexible, and adaptable labour force as a necessary condition for its long term good health. We also conclude that the responsibility of the private sector is to consider research and development outlays, and expenditures on personnel training not as costs that reduce the bottom line, but as investments in the long run welfare of the enterprise.

Uncertain Prospects: Trade Liberalization, the Economic Union and the Western Canadian Economy

4

In the 1990s, Western Canada will confront significant structural changes in its international trading relationships and, potentially, in its economic relationship with the rest of Canada. The consequences of these changes for the region's economy are unpredictable. The failure to ratify the Meech Lake Accord in the summer of 1990 brought into sharp focus differing perspectives on the structure of the Canadian economic union. At the very least, a more decentralized economic union may emerge and, at the worst, Canada as an integrated economic unit may cease to exist. Into this uncertain domestic environment now intrude structural changes in the international economy which may have significant effects on the economy of Western Canada.

Trade liberalization in the international economy, at least within regional blocks, is becoming increasingly evident. The Free Trade Agreement (FTA) with the United States has been operative since January 1, 1989, and negotiations are under way for a trilateral agreement including Mexico. In 1992 the European Economic Community will remove all internal trade barriers and restrictions on labour and capital movements among member countries. Multilateral trade initiatives are also ongoing. The Uruguay round of negotiations under the auspices of the GATT continues to focus on the contentious issue of agricultural subsidies.

All these trade initiatives are important from the perspective of the Western Canadian economy. But the magnitude of their contribution to economic growth in the West, indeed whether the contribution is positive or negative, depends also on salient features of the Canadian economic union. International trade is crucial to maintaining and increasing economic growth in the West. Yet as the previous chapters have shown, the structure of Western Canada's international trade has also led to an economy which exhibits significant volatility in a range of economic variables. How the regional economy and individuals cope with this volatility depends very much on the linkages of Western Canada with the rest of the country. That is, the economic union aspects of Confederation are very important in assessing the contribution of global trade liberalization to growth in Western Canada.

Two basic issues are addressed in this chapter. The first is abstract and concerns the contribution of an economic union such as Confederation to a regional economy with the characteristics of the West – an economy highly dependent on a narrow range of resource products with highly volatile prices whose exports are geographically concentrated. Here the focus is on the nature of the benefits of the Canadian economic union to a region with a structure of trade such as Western Canada's. The second issue concerns the nature of the structural changes ongoing in the international economy and their implications for Western Canada.

Confederation as an Economic Union

The literature on Confederation as an economic union draws heavily from international trade theory. The approach is to describe the various stages of economic integration possible among countries and to suggest the sources of real income gains as one moves to successively greater integration [Norrie et al. 1986]. The least degree of economic integration is that of a free trade area. In this arrangement the participating countries remove all barriers to trade in goods and services among themselves but each maintains its separate preagreement trade barriers with nonparticipating regions. The next stage of integration, a customs union, is merely a free trade area in which the participants agree to common trade barriers with the rest of the world. The next highest stage of integration, a common market, includes all of the features of a customs union with the further provision that all participants agree to the unhindered flow of capital and labour among member countries.

An economic union moves beyond the integration of output and factor markets into the integration of policy instruments by participating members. An economic union possesses all the characteristics of a common market, includes a monetary union and provides for harmonization, or integration, of policy instruments at a level compatible with the political structure chosen by participating members to allocate government functions. In the context of the Canadian economic union, there is a relatively high degree of decentralization of economic policy instruments to the participating provinces.

The Economic Surplus of Confederation

What then are the sources of economic gain from greater integration? Maxwell and Pestieau [1980:13-20] have provided a framework and explicit discussion of the sources of the potential economic surplus from an economic union. They outline four basic gains from the integration of factor and commodity markets and harmonization of policy instruments. These can be thought of as relative to a case in which the provinces were autarkic. The first set of gains are those which derive from incentives for greater specialization of labour and the exploitation of scale economies because of the elimination of barriers to interregional output and factor flows. The larger market of the economic union permits a more efficient allocation of labour and other factors between sectors and regions. The result is greater specialization, improved factor productivity, and higher real incomes.

The second source of economic surplus is a potential for the pooling of risks at the national level to ameliorate the consequences of regional instability. This pooling includes interregional insurance and transfer programs, labour, and capital flows between regions in response to varying economic opportunities, and macro stabilization policies aimed at specific regions. The ability to pool risks nationally is a highly valuable feature of an economic union. It permits regions to specialize in those areas of production in which they are most efficient while at the same time providing mechanisms of insurance against some of the costs of such specialization. In the short-term, the broader tax base of the economic union compared to the region permits transfers via the federal government from regions on the expansion phase of an economic cycle to those whose economies are in downturn. In the longer term, labour mobility is the ultimate insurance for those residents of regions whose economic base is in secular decline.

The sharing of overhead expenditures on joint projects such as defence, provision of justice, and large scale transportation projects is the third source of the surplus in the Maxwell-Pestieau framework. The final source of economic gain is the possible market power lacking for any region but possessed by an economic union in international trading relationships. Bigger and more diversified economies often appear to be more successful in trade negotiations because of both their sheer size and their ability to engage in more trade-offs given a more diversified economy. The use of power to obtain better market conditions improves the terms of trade experienced by the economic union and increases the aggregate real income of its residents.

The basic issue in evaluating the economic benefits of Confederation is whether benefits of similar or greater magnitude are available to the participating regions through alternate trading arrangements. The magnitude of the potential surplus derived from Confederation is not a constant. Its size will vary as a result of changes within Canada that influence the structure of the economy, the mechanisms of interregional adjustment, and external factors (foreign tariffs, transportation costs) that inhibit the possibility of trade with other countries.

Distributional considerations are also critical. They lie at the heart of "Western Alienation." From the perspective of any one region, it is not the size of the economic surplus accruing in aggregate to the economic union which is important. Paramount is the share of the economic surplus which the region receives, and the efficiency with which the institutional structure distributes the benefits of economic integration.

Structural Characteristics of Western Canada and the Surplus of Confederation

There are four outstanding features of the Western Canadian economy that emerge from the material outlined in the previous chapters. First, the region remains highly specialized in the production of natural resource products, and they dominate its exports. This structure is not surprising in light of natural endowments so that the venting of natural resource exports to international markets remains the economic engine of the region. Second, there is a high degree of geographic concentration of the West's major nongrain natural resource exports to the United States. Again, this result is not surprising in light of geography, transportation costs, and the high bulk-low value added characteristics of natural resource exports. Third, the prices of the West's natural resource products exhibit a significant degree of volatility, especially relative to import and consumer prices. Fourth, this volatility in natural resource prices is transmitted throughout the region's economy. A wide range of economic variables such as real GDP, employment, and personal income in the region exhibit significant volatility.

Given these structural characteristics, what can be said regarding the potential surplus of Confederation to the region? It is highly likely that two sources of the economic surplus – the gains from trade (with the rest of Canada) and the sharing of overheads – are less important from the perspective of the region. Trade with the international economy rather than with the rest of Canada is the major vehicle for capturing gains from specialization and scale. The FTA with the United States and the possibility of continued trade liberalization through multilateral vehicles such as GATT are mechanisms for preserving access to international markets. Moreover, to the extent that interregional trade in Canada is a consequence of remaining trade barriers (trade diversion), it may be quite costly relative to trade with external partners. The sharing of overheads may also no longer be an important source of economic gain to Western Canada. The logic of greater trade liberalization, especially the FTA, means that north-south linkages will increase in importance relative to the traditional east-west ones. There must be some doubt that the existing economic union is adequately structured to deal with this new spatial orientation.

The two remaining sources of economic surplus from Confederation – the insurance aspects and greater market power – are very important to the economic well-being of the residents of Western Canada. The highly volatile nature of the economy means that the economic stabilization, insurance, and transfer components of an economic union are critical. The narrow range of exports and their geographic concentration means that the West is highly susceptible to trade harassment from its major trading partners, especially the United States. Large trading partners can exercise market power to the detriment of smaller exporting regions.

Implications of Alternate Constitutional Scenarios for Western Canada

There are three basic constitutional scenarios that span the set of possible outcomes: the status quo, a revitalized Confederation, and independent regional economies, e.g. an independent Western Canada. The two major sources of economic surplus from integration relevant to Western Canada – market power to negotiate trade deals in international markets and insurance/stabilization clearly vary as one moves across these alternatives. We consider each in turn.

Market Power Issues

In the case of market power, there really is no distinction between the status quo and revitalized Confederation scenarios. The key question is whether the West would fare better as an independent entity or as part of the Canadian economic union. The evidence presented in earlier chapters depicts the Western Canadian economy as remaining highly specialized in a narrow range of resource and processed resource products destined for a geographically concentrated set of international markets. Had the West been an independent entity, it is quite likely that the softwood lumber dispute of 1986 would have ended with a countervail duty being imposed by the United States and the revenues accruing to the United States Treasury. The actual outcome – an export tax levied by the federal government as an interim measure until the provinces modified their timber pricing systems – reflects in no small measure the market power that a larger economy has in resolving trade disputes. A similar argument could be made in the potash antidumping case. The actual outcome was unfavourable from Saskatchewan's perspective, but it was probably better than would have been the case for a "stand alone" Western Canadian entity.

Western Canada, because of its pattern of trade and industrial structure, is almost uniquely situated to bear significant costs associated with American protectionist sentiments. Successful countervail and antidumping suits by United States producers, will be at the expense of resource producers, governments, and individuals in the West whose incomes derive from these sectors. The potential for Western Canadian resource producers to withstand successfully the exercise of monopsony power by the United States or other countries is greater within an economic union than outside of it. Trade harassment will still continue but the costs would be less for the West within the economic union than on its own.

The current discussions under the FTA regarding a common definition of subsidy, if successful, will probably lead to a better definition from the perspective of Western Canada than could be negotiated by the region as a separate entity. Moreover, it is by no means clear that a separate Western Canada would be a party to the FTA as it presently exists. Lipsey [1991] has argued it is unlikely that the FTA would remain intact were Canada to fragment. While the various Canadian regions would hope the Agreement remains in force, this outcome is by no means in the Americans' best interests, nor perhaps is it consistent with enabling legislation.

Insurance and Stabilization Issues

Western Canada is a highly volatile economy by virtually any measure, a characteristic derived from an industrial structure, specializing in the sale of price volatile products concentrated in a few export markets. This volatility is reflected in a range of macro variables, in mechanisms of adjustment to regional balance of payments shocks, such as shifts in relative prices within the region, and in interregional migration. Which of the constitutional scenarios best deals with this characteristic of the Western Canadian economy? A stand alone Western Canadian economy would likely exhibit greater volatility than that under the status quo, something that could be expected to change only over the long haul as capital formation was directed to broadening the economic base. It could be that a revitalized Confederation would best accommodate Western Canada's economic structure were policy instruments directed specifically at insurance and stabilization issues. The reasons for the claim that a stand-alone West be even more volatile than it is now, are varied. They stem in part from the argument that the West would forego many of the current avenues of interregional adjustment to economic shocks [Courchene, 1978]. Shifts in real income and wages, rather than adjustments through interregional migration and asset transfers through the national banking system, would become the dominant mechanism of adjustment. Income and unemployment variability would necessarily, as a result of more limited migration options, be greater in an independent West than they are now.

Perhaps more importantly, the West would forego the ability to pool risks nationally. The national industrial structure is more diversified than that for any one region. The ability of an independent West to provide economic stabilization would be much less than exists in Confederation currently because it lacks the diversified tax base to draw upon. Though the present institutional framework of Confederation does not deal very well with the problem of volatility exhibited by the West, a revitalized Confederation might do better. Designing unemployment insurance programs that were truly insurance programs rather than income maintenance schemes for declining regions and sectors, would be an integral element of reform. Constitutional change to ensure that federal transfer programs were automatically more responsive to cyclical regional economic conditions and less directed to preserving the spatial distribution of population in the long run would also be required. Federal policies promoting labour mobility and creating more efficient market based mechanisms of regional adjustment would further enhance the insurance/stabilization aspects of the economic union.

The ultimate insurance aspect of Confederation for the West remains access to the rest of Canada's labour markets in the event of a permanent decline in the region's terms of trade. What if, for example, if solar power become a commercial reality and the price of energy products plummets? The residents of a stand-alone West, particularly of an independent Alberta, would suffer a dramatic fall in living standards in the absence of access to the labour markets of other regions.

The importance of the Canadian economic union to the West cannot ignore the issue of the distribution of the economic surplus. A study undertaken for the Royal Commission on the Economic Union indicated that the current structure of Confederation generated a negative economic surplus [Whalley and Trela, 1986] and discriminated significantly against resource producing regions. While the conclusions of this study reflect its choice of a 1981 base year, and the distortions introduced into the energy sector by the since dismantled NEP, an array of federal policies remain which continue to dissipate portions (or all) of the gains from the economic union.

The International Trading Environment Facing Canada

In this section we review recent developments in global trade relationships and assess their implications for the West. Developments in the international trading environment offer the potential of greater trade liberalization. The most significant of these steps for Western Canada is the Canada-United States Free Trade Agreement operative since January 1, 1989. Negotiations are currently under way between the United States, Canada, and Mexico to create a continental free-trade agreement. The potential for the region's firms to access a truly continental market have never been greater. In 1992 the EEC will remove internal trade barriers and restrictions on labour and capital movements among member countries.

Multilateral trade negotiations under the auspices of the GATT – the Uruguay round – continue the efforts of earlier GATT rounds to promote trade liberalization. The Uruguay round also moves beyond a traditional focus on tariffs to address the contentious issues of agricultural subsidies and import restrictions, trade in services, and the dismantling of special trade regimes (textiles and clothing). These negotiations, especially if they lead to a resolution of the agricultural subsidy dispute between the United States and the EEC, could have a very positive outcome for Western Canadian grain producers. More generally, a liberalized trading environment could make it easier to sell Western Canadian products in international markets, and open the way to selling processed natural resource products, something that would contribute to longer stabilization in the economy.

Unfortunately, while the potential for trade liberalization and accompanying higher incomes and employment in Western Canada remains high, the possibility of increased trade barriers and greater balkanization of global trade cannot be dismissed. The FTA removes tariff barriers between Canada and the United States but leaves in place NTBs that restrict trade flows. Multilateral trade negotiations have made significant strides in reducing tariff barriers but most countries have been very ingenious in erecting a variety of nontariff barriers to protect domestic producers as tariff protection diminishes.

The General Agreement on Tariffs and Trade and Multilateral Trade Initiatives

The global economy has made remarkable strides through GATT in reducing the level of tariffs. In the case of Canada, the ratio of duty collected to total imports fell in 1945 from 11.1% and 11.3% for imports from all countries and United States, respectively, to 3.9 and 2.9%, in 1985 [Perry, 1989: 837]. Over the same period the percentage of imports entering Canada duty free from the United States and all countries increased by 31.4% and 18.1%, respectively [Perry, ibid]. Much of the decline in both the average rate of duty as well as in the range of commodities subject to duty reflects the results of the seven completed rounds of GATT, beginning with the first in 1947. For example, the Tokyo round of GATT negotiations which concluded in 1979 led to an average cut in Canada's trade-weighted base rate tariffs from 7.3% to 5.2% [Deardoff and Stern, 1991: 25]. A discussion of the institutional and administrative structure of GATT is beyond our scope here. Suffice to say the importance of GATT is that it sets out the broad legal framework governing global trading relationships and the manner in which individual countries can regulate imports and promote exports. It is the primary vehicle through which multilateral trade negotiations are conducted. Although GATT has been very successful in reducing tariff barriers on most manufactured commodities, certain commodities entering international trade have not fallen under the purview of GATT or, if they have, they have been largely outside GATT's regulatory framework.

The Uruguay round of GATT meetings is now focusing on these difficult areas which include trade in agricultural products, intellectual property, services, textiles and clothing, and tropical products. The institutional framework governing GATT is also under discussion including those articles dealing with safeguards (temporary restrictions on imports where domestic producers are seriously affected), dumping and countervailing measures (revisions to the subsidy code in terms of acceptable and unacceptable subsidy practices), and dispute settlement mechanisms. The current round of GATT meetings is very important to Western Canada for a number of reasons. If the Uruguay GATT meeting is successful in setting out rules for agricultural subsidies, it will end the costly agricultural subsidy war between the United States and EEC that has depressed grain prices received by prairie farmers and necessitated substantial subsidy payments to them. Success would eliminate the need for federal and provincial governments to fund these special programs aimed to help grain farmers squeezed financially by the international subsidy war. In Canada, the estimated producer subsidy equivalent [(the share of government program support to market income and program support for wheat rose from 18.4 to 51.8% from 1982 to 1986. The corresponding figures for the United States are 16.0 and 64.3%. [Economic Council of Canada, 1988: 22]. It has been estimated that subsidies for grain producers amounted to $6.2 billion over the period 1986-1989 inclusive [*Canadian Economic Observer*, May 1991: 3,5]. The pace of multilateral negotiations about subsidy rules also has implications for the Free Trade Agreement. It is highly unlikely there will much progress in these talks under the Canada-United States Free Trade Agreement until North American negotiators see the direction of multilateral negotiations on this question.

Another item of particular interest to Western Canada in the Uruguay round of meetings is improved market access (reduced nontariff barriers, or NTBs) for natural resource based products, including nonferrous metals and minerals, forestry products, and fish and fish products. NTBs include import quotas, voluntary export restraints, discretionary and nondiscretionary licensing, countervailing and antidumping investigations and duties, health standards, and export subsidies [Laird and Yeats, 1989: 15]. They hurt Western Canada by increasing uncertainty and reducing returns to traditional exports from the region. Perhaps more importantly, NTBs make it more difficult for Western Canada to promote further value-added in resource exports or to diversify into other nontraditional export products.

The recent study by Laird and Yeats [1989] calculates trade indices for major product groups affected by the NTBs of developed countries between 1966 and 1986, and highlights how pervasive NTBs are. The study shows that, in 1966, 4% of all countries' imports of agricultural raw products were affected by NTBs and that the share increased by 37% by 1986. For the EEC, the corresponding 1966 percentage and percentage point increase to 1986 are 3 and 24, respectively. For the United States, 14% of its agricultural raw material imports were affected by NTBs in 1966; this increased to 31 percentage points by 1986. In the case of total commodity imports by the EEC, 21% were subject to NTBs in 1966 and by 1986 the share had increased by 33 percentage points. The United States started off with a much greater proportion of its total commodity imports subject to NTBs in 1966 – 36% – but the increase of 9 percentage points by 1986 is much smaller than the corresponding figure for the EEC (Laird and Yeats, 1989, 13).

Canada-United States Free Trade: Motivation

While Canada has actively pursued multilateral trade initiatives through GATT, the most significant change in trading relationships emerged from bilateral negotiations with the United States. Two factors played a major role in Canada's efforts to negotiate a free trade agreement with the United States, and both are important in understanding the probable impact of the FTA on Western Canada.

The first factor was concern that Canadian manufacturing continued to lag in productivity in comparison to most industrialized countries. Evidence of a productivity gap was seen in the large Canadian trade deficit in manufactured goods (excluding automobiles) and low levels of and growth in most measures of productivity. The causes of this perceived productivity gap were subject to much debate. One school of thought viewed high levels of foreign ownership of Canadian manufacturing as the cause of its poor productivity performance. The competing view, and the one which came to dominate the subsequent policy debate especially after the release of the Report of the Royal Commission on the Canadian Economic Union and Development Prospects (The Macdonald Commission) in 1985, was that productivity failure reflected the joint impact of Canadian and foreign (basically American) tariffs on the structure of Canadian manufacturing. American tariffs were seen as forcing Canadian firms to rely mainly on the much smaller Canadian market for sales, while the Canadian tariff, by reducing import competition, created an environment of excessive product differentiation. The net result was too many different products produced in too few plants at too high a cost. Free trade between Canada and the United States was seen as the means of introducing competitive forces into the economy leading to the rationalization of Canadian manufacturing and greater productivity.

Concern over rising American protectionism in the 1980s was the second factor in the decision to pursue free trade with the United States. During the 1980s there was increased harassment of exporters to the United States. Soaring American trade deficits and increasing market penetration by imports prompted many industry groups to initiate countervail and antidumping suits. From 1980 to the first quarter of 1987, the United States initiated 4,172 countervail cases, 295 antidumping cases, and 1758 safeguard cases against Canada alone, on imports valued at over US$6 billion [Canada West Foundation,1988: 18]. Even when unsuccessful, these suits were still very costly for firms forced to defend themselves against charges of unfair trading practices. Moreover, the political environment in Congress became more receptive to the use of trade remedies legislation as a vehicle for extending protection to domestic producers in the face of what was perceived to be unfair foreign competition.

There is much evidence to suggest that the cause of United States trade problems was more the declining competitive position of American industry than the unfair trading practices of foreign firms. The United States had become a high-cost producer in a range of industries, especially natural resource products. A number of Canadian natural resource exports, including Atlantic fish, pork, shakes and shingles, and softwood lumber were the subject of contentious trade disputes with the United States between 1980 and 1985. The competitive problems stemming from a high-cost structure were further exacerbated by an appreciating United States dollar. For example, the American dollar in Canadian Dollars rose from 1.169 in 1980 to 1.404 in the first quarter of 1986 when protectionist pressures appeared to reach a peak in the United States. The high value of the American dollar made that country's exports more expensive and imports cheaper and led to a merchandise trade deficit of US$125 billion by the end of 1985.

The FTA: Potential Gains

The Free Trade Agreement, signed by the two governments on January 2, 1988, came into effect January 1, 1989. It is not the purpose of this paper to examine the FTA in detail. However, there are three key provisions in assessing its impact on Western Canada. The Provision calls for the phased removal of tariffs between Canada and the United States over a ten-year period with the highest tariffs being phased out over the longest period. The timetable set up in the Agreement for tariff removal has been accelerated in the case of some products. The second provision concerns energy; Canada gains secure access to the American market on a nondiscriminatory basis, while the United States gains more secure access to Canadian supplies in the event of world shortages. The third provision is a dispute settlement mechanism to evaluate whether the respective antidumping and countervailing duty laws of both countries are fairly applied. Either country may request a binational panel to review final antidumping or countervail determinations. During a seven-year period following the ratification of the FTA, both governments will attempt to arrive at a common definition of subsidy for application in their bilateral trade disputes.

The dispute settlement mechanism has been employed in a number of cases. The most important of these, from the perspective of the credibility of the process is the contentious case of Canadian pork exports to the United States. In May of 1989, the United States Department of Commerce, in a preliminary determination, ruled that Canada subsidized its hog producers and imposed duties of 3.5 cents a pound. This decision was upheld in final determination and the United States International Trade Commission also found that the alleged subsidies harmed the American pork industry. However, Canada successfully appealed the finding of subsidy and the imposition of countervail to the binational dispute-settlement panel. The United States then requested the formation of an "extraordinary challenge committee" to review the decision of the panel on the grounds that it had exceeded its jurisdiction. Fortunately, this subsequent committee, in June 1991, upheld the findings of the binational dispute settlement panel. The signal that emerges from the long, drawn-out pork case may be that, in the future, the weight of economic evidence rather than the political clout of a particular business lobby (the United States National Pork Producers Council) will become more important in any decision to launch a countervail petition.

There are widely varying estimates of the gains to Canada from entering into free trade with the United States. Early estimates suggested that GDP would increase by 7 to 10% and employment by 5.5% [Harris, 1985]. The Economic Council of Canada [1988] projected that, over 10 years, real GDP and employment would increase by 2.5% and 1.8%, respectively, as a result of the Free Trade Agreement. A recent study undertaken for the Economic Council by Muller and Williams [1989] finds that the Agreement could increase real incomes anywhere from 0.5% to 4.3% depending on assumptions regarding demand elasticities facing Canadian producers. Wigle [1988] estimated the real income gains to Canada for two scenarios. In the case where the alternative to free trade is simply a continuation of the status quo in trading relationships between the two countries, Canadian GDP increased by 0.8%. Where the alternative to free trade is a trade war, the gain to Canada of the FTA rose to 2.2%.

The most important factors in estimating real income and employment gains from the FTA is the magnitude of anticipated productivity gains and how they are incorporated into the analysis [Harris, 1985; Wigle, 1988]. The larger the productivity gains and the greater the rationalization of industry production (longer production runs) anticipated from the FTA, the greater are the real income gains projected. For example, the Economic Council of Canada [1988] projects that the FTA would increase Canadian GDP and employment by 0.7% and 0.5%, respectively, if productivity gains were absent and the only impact of the Agreement were price effects from tariff reductions. Hazeldine [1990, pp.791-806], in a simulation exercise, obtained welfare gains ranging from zero to more than 7% of GDP depending on assumptions regarding industrial structure and possible scale effects.

The Impact of the FTA on Western Canada

What of the impact of the FTA on Western Canada? In its simulation results the Economic Council of Canada [1988], inclusive of productivity gains, finds that for every Western Canadian province, the real income and employment gains exceed those for Canada, with Alberta gaining the most. The Canada West Foundation [1988], undertook a survey in January and February 1988, of approximately 100 trade associations and another 100 senior executive officers of major western Canadian companies. The results of the survey showed the following: (a) that industries accounting for 15.3% of employment in the region would be positively affected by the FTA, (b) industries accounting for 1.8% of employment would be adversely affected, and (c) a minimal affect on the remaining 83% of employment.

The Canada West study suggested that sectors accounting for 241,900 workers anticipated enhanced exports. Among these sectors were meat packing, livestock, freshwater fish processing, metal fabricating, electrical, petroleum and coal, nonmetallic minerals and chemicals. Moderate export benefits were anticipated in industries with 93,300 employees. Business services, including a range of computer/architectural/engineering/ consulting activities, accounted for 75,000 of these jobs. Another 178,900 jobs were located in sectors benefitting from greater export security to the United States. Chief among these industries was primary resource activity – oil and gas, and minerals. The FTA was anticipated to have negative effects on industries accounting for 59,500 jobs, including miscellaneous manufacturing (6,400 jobs), miscellaneous food processing (5,700 jobs), paper products (4,900 jobs), and poultry products (3,100 jobs) among others. The overwhelming majority of workers in Western Canada – some 2.8 million – are employed in industries where there will be no or, at best, minimal impact from the Agreement.

Other features of the FTA will undoubtedly have a positive impact on the Western Canadian economy but their effects will be difficult to quantify. For example, the FTA ensures that the federal government cannot, as it did under the National Energy Program, price energy at less than world prices, nor try to isolate Canadian energy consumers and producers from the direct influence of world energy price trends. The Agreement also requires that Canada be directly named in United States trade legislation passed subsequent to the FTA. Thus Canadian producers cannot be inadvertently "sideswiped" by American legislation aimed at countries such as Japan or others with whom the United States is in trade dispute.

In the longer run, successful negotiations for a common definition of subsidy may be one of the greatest benefits of the FTA. Such a definition would serve to shield Western Canadian resource producers from the worst excesses of American protectionism. The factors leading to trade disputes over Western Canadian resource exports to the United States still exist. A range of American resource industries continue to remain increasingly high cost producers because of depleting resource stocks and management practices [Percy and Yoder, 1987]. Unfortunately, within the American political environment these industries are well positioned to ensure that subsidy criteria and the United States trade dispute settlement procedures provide a high degree of protection. Lower cost producers (because of higher quality natural resources and more efficient production structures) are at risk. Thus the great need to agree upon a definition of subsidy which would incorporate unique features of some Western Canadian natural resource sectors – Crown ownership and management, and administrative pricing mechanisms. The issue of subsidy should turn on whether resource pricing and management practices are trade distorting and lead to injury of American producers. If the FTA yields a more tractable definition of subsidy than currently applied by the United States, it will have major long-term benefits to Western Canada by reducing the number of costly trade disputes.

The FTA: Some Cautions

Despite rhetoric regarding the economic consequences of the FTA which dominated the 1988 federal election, its direct impact on Canada, and Western Canada in particular, will neither be as dire as opponents argued, nor as beneficial as its advocates claimed. First, the tariff reductions are to be phased in over a ten-year period. Thus the impact in any one year of this ten-year phase is likely to be modest. Second, many estimates of the gains from the FTA are made in the context of bilateral trade flows alone. Studies that assess the impact of the FTA in the context of existing multilateral trade flows often find that lower overall gains from the Agreement occurs at the expense of other trading partners. In the case of Western Canada, this would mean some portion of increased exports to the United States would be foregone exports to the Pacific Rim or EEC. Similarly, increased imports from the United States might be at the expense of lower cost imports from elsewhere still subject to Canadian tariffs.

The issue of productivity gains is especially important from the perspective of Western Canada. Major Western Canadian industries relying on the United States market such as energy, softwood lumber, and potash are in the main already operating plants of minimum efficient size and are internationally competitive. Hence the direct effect of the FTA on such industries will be the price effects from removal of Canadian and American tariffs, and a more structured means of dealing with harassment.

⌐ .ndustry rationalization will be less important for most Western Canadian resource industries except perhaps in industries such as petrochemicals where, for some goods, production runs were too short. Schott [1988] has estimated that the impact of tariff cuts alone on United States imports from Canada will lead to an increase in Canadian exports of approximately 1985 US$1 billion. Of this total, $160 million consists of increased chemical exports, $75.5 million in primary metal exports, $16 million in oil and gas extraction, $12.3 in petroleum refining, and $14.9 million in paper and wood products. Thus the impact on Western Canada GDP and employment may be closer to the lower bound estimates of the Economic Council of Canada.

Canada-United States -Mexico Free Trade Negotiations

In June of 1991, Canada along with the United States and Mexico began serious negotiations to secure a continental free trade agreement. Canada's direct trade links with Mexico are modest in comparison to those with the United States. In 1988, Canada-United States trade amounted to $US150 billion, whereas Canada-Mexico trade totalled only $US1.5 billion, [Chambers and Percy, 1990: 5.

From Canada's perspective, the importance of the negotiations are much more closely linked to ensuring that the structure of the Canada-United States Free Trade Agreement also serves as the basis for more liberalized U.S-Mexico trade. In particular, the possibility of displacement of Canadian exports to the United States market, because of more favourable conditions of access granted Mexico under a bilateral agreement, requires that Canada be an active participant in negotiations. A United States-Mexico free trade agreement would require sectoral adjustments in the North American automobile, steel, and textile industries and it would clearly impinge on these industries in Canada. However, central Canadian firms are already experiencing greater competition in the American markets from Maquiladoras, customs-bonded assembly plants predominantly foreign-owned. The output of these plants are subject to special United States tariff rules under which all but the Mexican labour content and non-United States materials are subject to duty. A continental free trade agreement would at least provide a mechanism by which Canada would have some input to defining terms of access to the American market for Maquiladoras.

Western Canada's direct trade links with Mexico are also modest. The region's exports are concentrated in wheat and canola from the prairie provinces, sulphur from Alberta, and wood pulp from British Columbia. These four exports accounted for over 80% of Western Canada's exports to

Mexico in 1988 [Chambers and Percy, 1990: 6]. Within the United States market, Canadian producers do compete with Mexican exports in oil, live cattle, paper and paperboard, and zinc and they appear potentially competitive in natural gas and energy derivatives.

The benefits to Western Canada from an integrated North American market arise from three areas. The first is ensuring access to the United States market on a "level playing field" with Mexican producers especially with regards to energy-intensive products. Mexico continues to operate a two-tier energy pricing regime with domestic energy prices being lower than export prices. This pricing regime promotes greater domestic processing and provides a potential cost advantage to Mexican firms exporting such products to the U.S.. The provisions of the Canada-United States FTA preclude two-tier pricing regimes. Thus Western Canadian firms have a strong interest in ensuring that similar rules govern Mexican access to the American market.

Second, it is possible that successful tri-lateral negotiations would lead to an opening up of the Mexican energy sector. While it is highly unlikely that restrictions on foreign ownership of Mexican energy resources will be eliminated (it is part of the Mexican Constitution), it is quite possible that a much greater role for foreign firms in the exploration, development and service phases of energy production could emerge. Firms in Western Canada would be very well positioned to take advantage of these opportunities especially in light of Mexican unease regarding a too great American penetration of the energy sector.

Finally, consumers in Western Canada would benefit from lower prices especially in areas such as autos and textiles. However, the gains here are likely to be modest both in absolute terms and in comparison to the gains that had been anticipated from the Canada-United States FTA.

Managed Trade Vs. Free Trade

One final issue clouds the realization of gains from trade liberalization. Increasing, even maintaining export market shares for industries, such as those in the agricultural and natural resource sectors producing standardized or undifferentiated products, requires both cost leadership and a continuing commitment to introducing state of the art production methods. Yet in cases where Canadian industries have aggressively pursued expanding export volumes by increasing efficiency, such as in softwood lumber and potash, they have been hit with countervail actions by competitors in the United States.

The softwood lumber case is a classic example of an industry, especially in the British Columbia interior, that invested heavily in state-of-the-art production methods, and of how these cost savings, in conjunction with an appreciating United States dollar, led the industry's market share in the United States to reach 31.6% in 1985 [Percy and Yoder, 1987]. The result was a countervail suit, suspended once the Canadian federal government imposed a 15% export tax in lieu of increases in timber charges by provincial governments. This outcome, although benefiting the coffers of the provincial governments to whom the federal government remitted the export tax revenues, still penalized firms for enhancing their competitiveness.

Two other examples illustrate how in some instances market access is driven by market share rather than market forces. Canadian steel exports to the United States are not formally limited by quantitative restrictions as are other exports from other countries. Yet when Canadian steel exports exceed 3% of United States consumption, senators from steel producing states immediately raise the spectre of including Canadian steel imports under existing quota limits [Percy and Yoder, 1987: 10] The second example concerns Canadian plywood exports to the United States. In October of 1989, United States tariffs on tongued, grooved, and edgeworked plywood were reduced from 20% to 8%. The measure was technical in nature and unrelated to provisions of the FTA. Imports of these products presently account for a third of American consumption. The United States Administration sent a letter to the Canadian ambassador in Washington noting that an expansion of Canadian exports would lead the American government to rescind the tariff cuts. The United States Trade Representative, in a separate letter to a senator in the timber producing state of Montana, noted that Canada was warned that retaliation will follow a "diversion from normal patterns of trade" The letter continues ,"Simply put, our message was that if we see a diversion from normal patterns of trade, such that imports of this product increase significantly...we will take action to remedy this situation" [*Globe and Mail*, November 8, 1989].

The reality of Canada-United States trade (and trade among most industrialized countries) is that significant increases in market shares of imports, whether brought about by cost effectiveness, comparative advantage, exchange rate movements, or subsidies, will provoke a protectionist response in either country. The emergence of strong pressure groups from adversely affected industries or from regions where employment might be reduced by increased imports, usually means that increased import penetration provokes protection either as a stop-gap or as a permanent measure. Trade legislation has far more to do with domestic income distribution than it does with trade liberalization or economic efficiency.

Trade liberalization offers the potential of increased markets for Western Canadian producers, but aggressive pursuit of new trade opportunities especially in industries where export volumes are driven by price alone can lead to costly trade disputes. Managed trade with target market shares for imports, at least for some industries, seems to be the reality accompanying trade liberalization. The long-term benefit of the FTA may be that, if a common definition of subsidy is negotiated, market forces and comparative advantage rather than perceptions of what constitutes a "fair" market share may govern Canada-United States trade flows.

Europe 1992

The European Economic Community plans to eliminate all internal barriers to trade flows and labour and capital movements by 1992. The proposed reforms by community members are more ambitious than just the phasing out of intercountry customs and excise duties. The plans include harmonizing value-added taxes and increasing uniformity of income taxes, putting an end to nontariff barriers that arise from transportation requirements and product packaging, standardization of merger and take-over rules, liberalization of air and road transportation, banking and telecommunications access, and harmonization of technical standards covering a wide range of products. One study has estimated that the gains from these reforms could increase EEC GDP by CDN$400 billion within five years [Globe and Mail, April 18, 1988].

The result of these reforms will be an integrated market of 325 million people and a gross domestic product of 1987 US$4,303 billion [Wilkinson, 1989]. The Canada-United States trading block, by contrast, has a population of 270 million and a total gross domestic product of 1987 US$4,912 billion. The essential question that faces Western Canadian exporters to the EEC is whether the increased trade emerging among Community members as a result of the 1992 reforms will be open to rest of world countries or preserved for Community members through nontariff barriers. In theory it should be far less costly for Canadian firms to export to a single integrated market possessing common import requirements and technical standards. The reality is that some of the reforms, especially those which relate to harmonization of technical standards, offer wide scope for imposing NTBs to hamper access. The technical product standards , for example, can be designed to offer a distinct advantage to firms currently producing in the EEC. It is still too early to assess whether the 1992 reforms will lead to an open EEC or the emergence of a fortress Europe. However, it is likely that the response of many firms currently outside the Community will be to locate some production within the EEC rather than attempt to service such a large and prosperous market from Canadian plants. Thus the major effect of the EEC reforms may be to increase Canadian direct investment abroad rather than the volume of exports. This outcome would be especially true in the case of manufactured goods where marketing and advertising play a greater role in market penetration. In the case of agricultural and natural resource products, it is unlikely that European integration will have a significant impact on Western Canadian exports. The political forces which currently lead the EEC to impose such a wide range of NTBs on agricultural and resource imports are likely to be reinforced by integration rather than reduced.

Another factor which makes it likely that European integration will have at best only a marginally positive impact on Western Canada is the effort of the EEC to increase the degree of integration which currently exists with the six countries of the European Free Trade Association (EFTA). At least in the short-term, EFTA members may be better placed to capture the gains from EEC integration especially if their trade links with the Community are strengthened. The EFTA countries include Sweden and Finland, both significant export competitors of Western Canada.

Trade Liberalization and Western Canada: Promoting Structural Change?

It is highly unlikely that trade liberalization will lead to any major shift in the industrial structure of the western provinces. Quite the reverse could be true. The FTA and successful negotiations for a continental free agreement including Mexico will likely reinforce the region's comparative advantage in and the relative importance of the natural resource and agricultural sectors to provincial incomes. Greater specialization rather than diversification of industrial structure is the logical outcome of trade liberalization in the absence of any fundamental change in managerial attitudes. To the extent that trade liberalization reinforces the existing pattern of economic specialization in Western Canada, it will be accompanied by greater economic instability. The region's current structure of exports is highly concentrated in commodities whose prices are highly volatile, and further specialization in these products will increase the degree of volatility transmitted to the rest of the economy. Moreover, the FTA, in the absence of successful multilateral trade initiatives, may lead to even greater geographic concentration of Western Canada's exports and hence reinforce the instability emanating from the pattern of product specialization. But the jury on this is still out for it could possibly also create new markets for Western Canadian processed, value-added goods.

The Economic Union and Trade Liberalization

On one hand, trade liberalization offers Western Canadian producers more secure access to international markets and the possibility of increased exports. Both factors should contribute to increasing real incomes of residents of the region. On the other hand, trade liberalization may exacerbate the degree of economic instability in the West and also leave the region open to the exercise of market power by its major trading partners if the geographic concentration of exports increases.

For reasons discussed in the first part of this chapter, a strong case can be made that the greatest benefits of trade liberalization for the West can be achieved in the context of a revitalized economic union. Two factors are of critical importance. First, the economic union offers the potential of insurance against the consequences of instability arising from specialization in natural resource and agricultural products. In the short-term this insurance takes the form of a more diversified tax base and the means of financing transfer payments. In the long-term the economic union offers insurance for individuals against the consequences of a permanent decline in the region's terms of trade. Economic opportunity through interprovincial migration represents a secure hedge against the vicissitudes of a resource based economy.

Second, Canada as an economic union has more clout in international trade negotiations than any one region would possess on its own. The benefits of size for Canada as an economic unit in the negotiating process ought to be reflected in two outcomes. First, the agreements are more likely to achieve objectives of the various Canadian regions than otherwise would have been the case. It seems highly unlikely than any individual region as a stand-alone unit would have been able to negotiate the dispute settlement mechanism of the FTA or have had the opportunity to secure a common definition of subsidy to regulate trade with the United States. Second, Canada as a larger entity has the ability to enforce the provisions of agreements or to ameliorate adverse decisions of the authorities regulating trade. The example of the softwood lumber case is worth repeating. The outcome of Canada imposing an export tax was certainly preferable to the alternative of the United States imposing a countervail duty. Would British Columbia as an independent entity have been successful in achieving this outcome? One will never know but it is unlikely that the province would have escaped the imposition of a countervailing duty on its softwood lumber exports to the United States.

The implications of trade liberalization for Western Canada cannot be separated from the region's economic linkages with the rest of Canada. From this perspective and for the reasons that we have stated, trade liberalization within a revitalized economic union is a preferable scenario, especially when compared to those which restrict the degree of economic integration including labour mobility between the region and the rest of Canada. This is not to say that the status quo in the economic union as presently constituted is ideal for the West.

There are problems. The economic surplus is smaller than it might be, and that surplus is inequitably distributed; the current structure of fiscal federalism accents too much a preservation of the economic size of regions in secular decline, and insufficiently addresses the unique needs of a cyclically unstable region like the West, one that remains surprisingly dependent on, and specialized in, the exploitation and utilization of its natural resource base. Resource markets are sensitive to trade disputes, are volatile, and that variability underlines the mechanisms of adjustment to economic shocks. Our conclusion is that for the federation to work more strongly in the West's interest, constitutional change must provide structures that assure

(a) more effective provision for insurance/stabilization measures in the economic union;

(b) labour mobility;

(c) realization of the market power advantages inherent in a united Canada.

5 Whither the West?

In 1984, the Economic Council of Canada, in a major study of Western Canada, Western Transition, reviewed prospects for the region, noting two general views regarding the long-run economic growth of resource-based economies. One view coupled growth prospects tightly to market opportunities for the resource base. This view, "the resource growth and retrenchment school" (p. 33), offers little in the way of optimism for efforts to broaden industrial structure, and, by inference, is very pessimistic regarding the longer-run outlook of those regional economies dependent upon nonrenewable resources, or those which poorly manage renewable resources.

The other view, "the growth and evolution school," is far more sanguine regarding the possibilities of market-based diversification in resource-based economies and longer-run economic prospects. In particular, the Economic Council viewed manufacturing and services, especially the latter, as lessening dependence on natural resources as a source of Western Canadian economic growth. In our study, we are less optimistic regarding market-based diversification in the absence of a significant change in business attitudes to product development and market expansion. For us the evidence suggests that, while unprocessed and processed natural resource exports maintain Western Canada's high standard of living, and will continue to do so in the future, the mind-set and known risk factors in resource-based organizations may unduly tilt planning and investment priorities to continued resource exploitation. That is, the sources of market-based diversification anticipated by the Economic Council may not materialize, or may emerge only when growth prospects for natural resources are dismal. At that point, it may well be very difficult for market-based diversification to occur.

A brief summary of the main conclusions of each of the four chapters of the study will make clear why we view the coming decade as posing both significant challenges and opportunities in expanding the breadth of the region's exports and address the problem of instability.

The chapter, "Profiles," reported global trading relationships of the four western provinces and the region as a whole, considered the relative importance of export products, and identified their geographic markets. From 1986 to 1989, exports originating in Western Canada accounted for from 23 to 30% of national merchandise exports, and if the export trade in motor vehicles and parts are excluded (virtually all of which represent multinational transborder transactions) then the figure is 38%. Provincial export shipments varied from 13 to slightly more than 29% of provincial GDP with direct export shares to the international economy highest in British Columbia and lowest in Manitoba.

About $2 in every $3 of the region's exports to the rest of the world are accounted for by 14 commodities, and, of that $2 dollars, about $1.25 represents the shipment of unprocessed raw materials. Among the four provinces, the exports of Alberta and Saskatchewan contain the higher proportion of unprocessed materials.

Spatial markets for Western Canadian exports are considerably different in relative importance than for the country as a whole. About 55% of the region's exports go to the United States compared with a national figure in excess of 75%. Most importantly, Canada's export markets in Japan and other Pacific Rim countries are almost entirely western based. Particularly strong links between British Columbia and the Pacific Rim countries is evident with shipments to this region accounting for some 30% of the province's international market.

The main conclusion of "Profiles" is that, despite some interprovincial differences in the commodity composition of exports and their international markets, all western provinces are highly integrated into global trade flows, through exports of a few relatively unprocessed natural resources.

The second chapter, "Instability, Commodity Price Volatility, and the Exchange Rate," examines links between Western Canada's exports and the high degree of economic instability which characterizes the region. The evidence indicates that three of the four western provinces, the exception being Manitoba, display a much higher degree of instability in broad measures of economic activity, such as personal income, than do provinces in central Canada or the Atlantic region. An obvious inference is that this instability derives in part from the composition of Western Canada's exports. The evidence shows marked swings in the prices of key primary product exports. The high degree of volatility is apparent from a standard measure of price change showing that agricultural prices are almost 12 times more volatile than the Consumer Price Index, and rates of change in forest product, energy, and metals prices are respectively in the order of 5 times greater.

Yet volatile commodity prices are only part of the explanation for the high degree of overall economic instability displayed by the Western Canadian economy. Adding to this volatility has been that in the external value of the Canadian dollar – the exchange rate. Movements in the rate have a direct impact on the profit margins of export producers. In theory, a fluctuating exchange rate can help smooth out swings in primary product prices, with depreciation offsetting the adverse impact on producers of falling commodity prices, and appreciation helping to keep the economy from overheating from sharply rising commodity prices.

In assessing the role of the exchange rate in volatility, measures of the the exchange rate must incorporate (i) the importance of individual international markets to Western Canada, and (ii) the effect of cross rates on direct competition as well as on country competition in third markets. IMF indexes of real and effective exchange rates, and new WCER indexes of real and nominal exchange rates, meet these standards, but the Bank of Canada's G-10 index of nominal effective exchange rates does not. Both the IMF and the Western Centre's indexes show that exchange rate movements during much of the period since the mid-seventies have been destabilizing in their impact on the Western economy. Exchange rate movements adjusted for price change, i.e. percentage changes in the real exchange rate, exacerbated the boom-followed-by-bust conditions from 1976 through early 1984, though the exchange rate did moderate the effect on Western Canada of the sharp increase in commodity prices that occurred in 1987 through the onset of the 1990 recession.

Thus the evidence is that three of the four Western provincial economies are significantly more unstable that others in Canada. This instability is linked to the region's global trade through at least two channels. The first is the high degree of price volatility displayed by the region's main commodity exports. The second is that procyclical nature of movements in the real exchange generally exacerbated rather than ameliorated swings in economic activity.

The third chapter, "Buffers and Strategic Options," reviewed existing mechanisms for coping with instability and advanced longer-run strategic options for addressing this problem. The current institutional and program mechanisms, which to a degree modify adverse shocks, apply primarily to the agricultural and energy sectors. Questions can, however, be raised about the possible adverse impacts of their design in inhibiting sectoral adjustments to changing market realities.

The chapter classifies the region's exports to the international economy in terms of "old" and "new" products and markets. Not only are the region's exports highly concentrated and unprocessed, but seen from this vantage they are largely in the old product/old market cell, a position which increases vulnerability – for an already volatile Western economy – to a range of issues from the environment, through the aspirations of LDCs and NICs, to economic restructuring, to the growing prevalence of managed trade. Against the backdrop of these issues, positioning in the old/old cell confronts private sector exporters with a potentially formidable array of problems.

For our traditional resource-based exporters, under competitive threat from low wage, offshore producers, cost leadership through process innovation – "cutting, digging, reaping" not more but more efficiently – is the rational strategy. This will require companies to adopt more capital intensive operations and result not only in declining shares of the region's employment in these industries, but also that future job opportunities will demand more technical training and higher skill levels.

However, the strategy of cost leadership even when successfully applied is still not the answer for at least two reasons. First, it leaves the region unduly exposed, because of its narrow export base, to the impacts of technical change on product demand. Second, the exports of low-cost producers (as our forest industry well knows) are often subject to countervail suits in an era of managed trade.

The challenge for the private sector is to create a broader export base by finding new spatial markets for exports, or by building added customer value into the activities in which the region is internationally competitive. Adding value to what we produce means tailoring what we now do to customer needs. That will require not simply more research and development expenditures, but new combinations of technology, marketing capability, product quality, and labour skills. Setting future priorities to enter new markets and develop new products means that traditional resource firms will be exposed, not to the more familiar forms of exploration and development risks, but to unfamiliar risks related to the behaviour of competitors and buyers in an entirely different type of market place.

The most important role that government can play in all this is to create a supportive climate, one that facilitates change. One set of policies should aim at transfer of knowledge into the export base by

1. encouraging exporters to add value to their products to take maximum advantage of the Free Trade Agreement;

2. funding a first class educational system as the prime source of a high quality labour force needed for diversification;

3. supporting a continuing collaborative structure involving industry, government and universities for transferal to the private sector of technology generated by research and development and market analysis.

A further set of policies should aim at smoothing cycles in business activity in these volatile economies, and at changing the tax system to permit fast write-offs and deductions thereby reducing penalties on the highly risky returns from startup investments.

The final chapter, "Uncertain Prospects: Trade Liberalization, the Economic Union, and Western Canadian Economy," assesses the impact on the region of greater international trade liberalization, and the place of the west within the economic union. The potential for the Western Canadian economy to increase exports and improve the standard of living of its residents has never been higher. Most significant is the Canada-United States Free Trade Agreement. In the next decade, the removal of tariff barriers will benefit consumers through lower prices, and increase the productivity of Western Canadian firms by both enhancing and ensuring greater access to the American market. The gains to the region may be as high as 2.5% of the region's GDP over 10 years should productivity gains accompany increased North-South trade flows. However, if the main effects of the Agreement are only those arising from the price effects of tariff removal, the gain may only be about 0.5% over the decade.

At the same time that incentives for North-South trade flows have increased, federal and provincial governments in Canada are attempting to reduce interprovincial trade barriers. Thus, the potential for Western Canadian firms to access a truly continental market is in place.

There are also forces operative for trade liberalization beyond North America. Multilateral trade negotiations under the auspices of GATT – the Uruguay round – continue the efforts of earlier GATT rounds to remove tariffs as a barrier to trade. The Uruguay round moves beyond the traditional focus on tariffs and addresses contentious issues of agricultural subsidies and import restrictions, trade in services, and the dismantling of special trade regimes (textiles and clothing). Though progress has been slight thus far, these negotiations, especially if they were to lead the United States and the EEC to resolve their agricultural trade subsidy war, could have a very positive effect on Western Canadian grain producers.

In 1992 the EEC will remove internal trade barriers and restrictions on labour and capital movements among member countries. The result will be the largest integrated market in the world. The potential for increased exports from Western Canada is good if the EEC remains outward looking in its trade orientation.

Unfortunately, while the potential for trade liberalization and accompanying higher incomes and employment in Western Canada remains high, the possibility of increased trade barriers and greater balkanization of global trade is also significant. The Free Trade Agreement removes tariff barriers between Canada and the United States but leaves in place a formidable array of nontariff barriers that restrict trade flows. The long term success of the Agreement from the perspective of Western Canada may well hinge on success in current negotiations over a common definition of "subsidy" to serve as the basis for resolving countervail and antidumping suits between the two countries.

The chapter concludes with the view that the key structural problems we have identified – a concentration of exports in unprocessed natural resources and unstable regional economies – will remain or, at worst, be intensified by trade liberalization. Under the Free Trade Agreement there is, in the absence of changes in business attitudes, the very strong possibility of even greater specialization in unprocessed natural resource exports, and even more spatial concentration in traditional export markets. Fundamental changes in product diversification, the spatial distribution of export markets, and marketing strategies will emerge only as a consequence of a change in business attitudes, and in a climate fostered by government that encourages greater risk taking in the private sector .

Appendices

Appendix A

Spatial Market Shares in Some Important Western Canadian Exports
(1986-88 averages, value basis)

Western Canadian Product	Region/Country Market	Share of Spatial Market
(1) Crude Oil	US	100.0
(2) Natural Gas	US	100.0
(3) Softwood Lumber	US	70.1
	Japan	16.8
	E E C	9.9
	Australia	1.9
(4) Woodpulp	US	32.6
	E E C	23.3
	Japan	19.24
	Other Pacific Rim	8.0
	Latin America	2.5
(5) Newsprint	US	72.2
	Japan	2.6
	E E C	7.2
	Australia	2.5
	Other Pacific Rim ex China	3.9
	China	1.2
	Latin America	2.5
(6) Wheat	USSR	28.9
	China	21.3
	Latin America	17.0
	Japan	14.3
	E E C	11.3
	Other Pacific Rim e.g. China	6.1
(7) Coal	Japan	72.9
	South Korea	12.9
	Latin America	4.4
	Other Pacific Rim	2.8
(8) Potash	US	60.0
	Japan	8.3
	Latin America	6.7
	South Korea	4.6
	E E C	3.3
	China	8.6
	Other Pacific Rim	1.9
	Australia	2.9
(9) Sulphur	Latin America	30.0
	U S S R	11.4
	E E C	10.1
	US	10.0
	South Korea	9.7
	Australia	8.6
	Taiwan	3.3
(10) Rapeseed	Japan	84.0
	Latin America	12.9
	E E C	2.2

Appendix B

Composition of the Western Canada Commodity Price Index

Commodity	Data Source	Weight
Wheat,Spring No. 1, Minneapolis	Producer Price Index US Bureau of Labor Statistics	.1081
Barley, No. 3, Minneapolis	Producer Price Index US Bureau of Labor Statistics	.0121
Thermal coal	Industry Products Price Index Statistics Canada	.0771
Crude petroleum	Producer Price Index US Bureau of Labor Statistics	.1919
Natural gas	Producer Price Index US Bureau of Labor Statistics	.1123
Douglas fir, new, dressed	Producer Price Index US Bureau of Labor Statistics	.1708
Newsprint, standard	Producer Price Index US Bureau of Labor Statistics	.0432
Woodpulp, chemical sulphate bleach	Producer Price Index US Bureau of Labor Statistics	.1206
Aluminum, ingots	Producer Price Index US Bureau of Labor Statistics	.0194
Copper, refined	Producer Price Index US Bureau of Labor Statistics	.0231
Nickel, alloy mill shapes	Producer Price Index US Bureau of Labor Statistics	.0056
Zinc, slab prime western	Producer Price Index US Bureau of Labor Statistics	.0077
Fish, Pacific Coast, canned salmon	Industry Products Price Index Statistics Canada	.0210
Potash	Average contract price, US$ Canpotex	.0299
Sulphur	Average contract price, US$ Cansulex	.0298

Appendix C

Country Weights in the G-10 Nominal Effective Exchange Rate Index
of the Bank of Canada

Country	Weight
United States	.8180
West Germany	.0240
Belgium	.0090
France	.0140
Italy	.0120
Japan	.0600
Netherlands	.0110
Sweden	.0050
Switzerland	.0050
United Kingdom	.0420

Source: *Bank of Canada Review*

Weights represent averages for the period 1972 - 1986.

Appendix D

Country Weights in the International Monetary Fund Nominal and Real Effective Exchange Rate Indexes

Country	Weight
Austria	.0085
Belgium	.0104
Denmark	.0077
France	.0465
West Germany	.0503
Italy	.0384
Japan	.0711
Netherlands	.0145
Norway	.0056
Sweden	.0164
Switzerland	.0081
United Kingdom	.0195
United States	.6420
Australia	.0367
Finland	.0093
Ireland	.0030
Spain	.0122

Source: J.R. Artus and A.K. McGuirk, "A Revised Version of the Multilateral Exchange Rate Model", *International Monetary Fund Staff Papers*, 1981, Vol. 28, pp. 305-6.

Appendix E

Effective Exchange Rate Indexes for Western Canada

An effective exchange rate index is composed of a weighted basket of currencies with choice of weights determined by the objectives to be served. The primary purpose of the reported Western Canadian effective exchange rate index is to evaluate changes in the region's international competitiveness.

The choice of currency basket, determined by practical considerations, includes the OECD countries plus Korea. These countries taken together account for a significant share of Western Canadian exports as is apparent in Chapter 1. However, there are a number of missing currencies, including China, the former USSR, and the Latin American countries, where exports are of some significance to the West. These are countries either with nonconvertible currencies, or with problems bordering on hyperinflation. By excluding these countries from the index, the implicit assumption is that the average for the convertible currencies included in the basket is a valid measure of the behaviour of the nonconvertible and other excluded currencies. Since the main purpose of the WCEER index is to gauge competitive position with respect to exports, a bilateral weighting system (like that in the Bank of Canada's G-10 index) is unsuitable. A more complete measure of competitiveness in export markets requires that third country effects be taken into account. The WCEER index by employing multilateral weights is effectively "double weighted." The weight assigned a given country in the currency basket is estimated in the following sequence:

(a)   identify a set of commodities representative of Western Canada's dominant exports; these are wheat, canola, barley, crude oil, natural gas, woodpulp, sawn coniferous lumber, newsprint and paperboard, copper ores and concentrates, zinc ores and concentrates, potash, and sulphur;

(b)   take each commodity and derive for each country a set of market shares (including home supplies and imports from other countries) in the currency basket; the result is a country matrix of market share weights for each commodity;

(c)   take Western Canada's exports of each commodity and calculate the set of country export share ratios; the result is a vector of export weights for each commodity;

(d)   the country weight for each commodity is then determined by multiplying the matrix of market share weights by the vector of export weights and adjusting the sum of the products to unity;

(e)   the aggregate country weight (i.e. the country weight with all commodities considered) is obtained from the sum of the following products: individual country weights for each commodity multiplied by the given commodity's share in the aggregate value of the designated set of export commodities.

The aggregate country weight is multiplied by the exchange rate of each foreign currency in the basket per Canadian dollar (in index form), and the product summed across all countries yields the nominal effective exchange rate index.

The WCER real effective exchange rate index is obtained by deflating the nominal index by the ratio of each country's CPI to the Canadian CPI.

The country weights in the indexes are as follows:

United States	.6209
Australia	.0955
Japan	.0830
U K	.0487
Sweden	.0245
France	.0233
West Germany	.0189
Italy	.0154
Korea	.0104
Finland	.0094
Norway	.0080
New Zealand	.0076
Portugal	.0075
Spain	.0074
Belgium-Luxembourg	.0058
Netherlands	.0050
Switzerland	.0030
Austria	.0029
Denmark	.0028

Weights derived from 1986 and 1987 data.

Appendix F

Results from a Regression Model Relating Western Canadian Employment to Commodity Real Prices and the Real Exchange Rate

Dependent Variable:
Quarterly percent change in monthly average Western Canadian seasonally adjusted employment.

Independent Variables:

(a) Quarterly percent change in monthly average real commodity prices (DCPR).

(b) Quarterly percent change in monthly average real effective exchange rates (DWCR).

Period Covered:
Fourth quarter of 1976 to the second quarter of 1991.

Variable	Lag	Coefficient	T-statistic
DCPR	0	0.05464	1.864
DCPR	1	0.08910	3.062
DCPR	2	0.04962	1.614
DWCR	0	-0.03249	-0.706
DWCR	1	-0.07018	-1.518
DWCR	2	-0.10445	-2.156
Constant	0	0.45565	5.597
Rho	1	0.22532	1.5119

R^2=0.450   Adj R^2=0.373   Standard Error of Estimate=2.5497
SSR=16.42   Durbin-Watson=1.576

Summary of the impact of DCPR for lags 0 to 2
Summation of coefficient values = 0.1933
T-statistics = 4.048   Significance level = .0005

Summary of the impact of DWCR for lags 0 to 2
Summation of coefficient values = -0.2071
T-statistics = 2.563   Significance level = .0134

Data on employment from Statistics Canada, *Historical Labour Force Statistics* (72-001).

Real exchange rate and commodity price data from the Western Centre for Economic Research.

B ibliography

Agriculture Canada (1987). *Canada's trade in agricultural products*, 1984, 1985 and 1986, (pp 15, 38-42). Ottawa: Minister of Supply and Services Canada.

Agriculture Canada (1987), *Series of agricultural initiatives announced*, News Release Ottawa; Communications Branch.

Alberta. (1985), *Position and policy statement on enhancing the Alberta capital market*, September 1985.

Alberta.(1984). *Proposals for an industrial and science strategy for Albertans 1985-1990*, (White Paper).

Alberta. (1985). *Submission to the Grain Transportation Agency - The Western Grain Transportation Act Review*.

Alberta. Treasury Department (1987). *Alberta Heritage Trust Fund Annual Report 1986-1987*.

Anderson, David L, (1986). *An analysis of Japanese coking coal procurement policies: The Canadian and Australia Experience*. Kingston, Queen's University, Centre for Resource Studies, Queen's University.

_____. (1985, July) "Market Power and the Saskatchewan Potash Industry", *Canadian Public Policy*, pp. 321-328.

_____. (198?). *The Saskatchewan potash industry: Alternative strategies for future development*, (Discussion paper no. 264). Ottawa: Economic Council of Canada.

Artus, Jacques R., Anne Kenny McGuirk (1981). *A revised version of the multilateral exchange rate model* (International Monetary Fund Staff Papers, Volume 28, pp. 305-6) Place: International Monetary Fund.

Barber, Clarence L.(1983, September) *On the form and presentation of the Government of Manitoba's budget, Western Economic Review*,2(2), pp. 52-71.

Barber, Clarence L., (1966). *The Theory of Fiscal Policy as Applied to a Province,* Toronto: Ontario Committee on Taxation, Queen's Printer.

Belanger, Gerard (1976). *An Indicator of Effective Exchange Rages for Primary Producing Countries.* (International Monetary Fund Staff Papers, Volume 23, 1976, pp. 113-136). Place: International Monetary Fund.

Bhagwati, J. (1987) . *Services.* In Finger, J. M. and A. Olechowski (eds.). *The Uruguay Round: A Handbook on the Multilateral Trade Negotiations.* World Bank, Washington D.C. pp. 207-216.

Brown, M. & B. McKern. (1987) *Aluminum, copper and steel in developing countries.* Paris: Development Centre Studies, OECD.

Canada West Foundation. (1988). *Evaluating the fine print...The Free Trade Agreement and Western Canada.*

Carmichael, Edward A. (1986). *New stresses on confederation: Diverging Regional Economies* (Observation No. 28)Toronto: C.D. Howe Institute, Toronto, June 1986.

Carmichael, Edward A., & Katie Macmillan. (1988) *Focus and follow-through: Policy Review and Outlook,* Toronto: C.D. Howe Institute.

Chambers, Edward J. (1991). *Indexes of Effective Exchange Rates for Western Canada* (Information Bulletin No. 2) Edmonton: University of Alberta, Western Centre for Economic Research.

Chu, K.Y. & T.K. Morrison (1986) "World Non-Oil Primary Commodity Markets," *(International Monetary Fund (IMF) Staff Papers* pp 139-184). Place: International Monetary Fund.

Collins, A.F. (1980,February). "The Alberta Heritage Savings Trust Fund: An Overview of the Issues." *Canadian Public Policy,* pp. 158-165.

Condlin, David W. & F. St.Hilaire (1988) *Canadian high-tech in a new world economy: A case study of information technology.* Montreal: Institute for Research on Public Policy.

Constantino, L., & M. Percy (1988) *The Political Economy of Canada - U.S. Trade in Forest Products* (Discussion Paper). Vancouver: Forest Economics and Policy Analyses Research Unit, the University of British Columbia.

Courchene, Thomas (1978). "Avenues of Adjustment: The Transfer System and Regional Disparities," in *Canadian Confederation at the Crossroads: The Search for a Federal-Provincial Balance.* Vancouver: Fraser Institute.

Dertouzos, M., R. Lester & R. Solow (1989) *Made in America* Cambridge, MA., The MIT Press, 1989.

Dutton, J. & T. Grennes (1987) "Alternative measures of effective exchange rates for agricultural trade," *European Review of Agricultural Economics* **14-4,** pp. 427-442.

Drucker, Peter F. (1987, January) "Dramatic Shifts in the Global Economy." *Dialogue* **75,** pp. 2-7.

Economic Council of Canada (1988). *Handling the Risks* Ottawa: Supply and Services Canada.

_____. (1988) *Venturing Forth* Ottawa: Supply and Services Canada.

_____ (1984). *Western Transition.* Ottawa: Supply and Services Canada.

Finlayson, J. & M. Zacher (1988). *Commodity trade: The harsh realities* Ottawa: The North South Institute.

Helliwell, J.F, M.E. MacGregor, & A. Plourde (1984) "Energy policy and industrial activity: A reply," *Canadian Public Policy* **10 (4),** pp. 476-480.

Helliwell, J.F., M.E. MacGregor, R.N. McRae, & A. Plourde (1987). *Oil and gas taxation in Canada: An analysis of developments since the Royal Commission on Taxation* (Energy Study No. 87-2) Toronto: Institute for Policy Analysis.

Howitt, Peter (1986). *Monetary Policy in Transition: A Study of Bank of Canada Policy, 1982-1985, Policy Study No. 1* Toronto: C.D. Howe Institute.

International Monetary Fund (IMF) (1988). *Commodity Market Developments and Prospects* Washington, DC.

Ingram, W.H. ((1983) *The Alberta sulphur industry: An economic and marketing analysis* Unpublished master's thesis, University of Alberta, Edmonton, Alberta.

Kerr, W.L. (1985). "The changing economies of the western livestock industry." *Canadian Public Policy,* pp. 294-300.

Koch, Elmar B. (1984). *The Measurement of Effective Exchange Rates.* (Working Paper No. 10). Bank for International Settlements.

Laird, S. & A. Yeats, (1989). "Non-tariff barriers of developed countries, 1966-86," *Finance and Development,* pp. 12-13.

Lane, Hon. J. Gary (1986, March) Presentation by the Minister of Finance, Province of Saskatchewan, *Budget Address.*

Lipsey, Richard G., & Murray G. Smith (1986, June). *Global imbalances and U.S. policy responses: A Canadian perspective* paper presented at a meeting sponsored by The C.D. Howe Institute, Toronto, and the National Planning Association, U.S.

Mansell, R., & M. B. Percy (1990) *Strength in Adversity: A study of the Alberta economy*, (Western Studies in Economic Policy, Volume I), Toronto: C.D. Howe Institute, and the Edmonton: Western Centre for Economic Research.

Maxwell, Judith & Caroline Pestieau (1980). *Economic Realities of Contemporary Confederation*, (Accent Quebec 14). Montreal: C. D. Howe Research Institute.

McMillan, M.L., M.B. Percy & L.S. Wilson (1984). "Proposals for an industrial and science strategy for Albertans 1985 to 1990: Innovative or wishful thinking?" in Walker, Michael A.(ed.) *Focus on Alberta's Industrial and Science Strategy Proposals* (pp. 27-65)Vancouver: The Fraser Institute.

Mintz, J.(1988). "An empirical estimate of corporate tax refundability and effective tax rates," *Quarterly Journal of Economics*, **(1)** pp. 225-232.

Muller, R. A. & J. R. Williams *A general equilibrium analysis of the Canadian-United States Bilateral Trade Agreement* (Discussion Paper No. 364) Ottawa: Economic Council of Canada.

Norrie, Kenneth H. (1983, December)."Not much to crow about: A primer on the statutory freight rate issue," *Canadian Public Policy* IX(4), pp. 434-445.

Norrie, Kenneth, Richard Simeon & Mark Krasnick (1986). *Federalism and the Economic Union*, (Research Studies of the Royal Commission on the Economic Union and Development Prospects for Canada 56). Toronto: University of Toronto Press.

OECD (1988). *Innovation Policy: Western Provinces of Canada*, Paris: OECD.
_____(1987). *National Policies and Agricultural Trade: Country Study Canada*, Paris: OECD.

Percy, Michael B., & Christian Yoder, (1987). *The Softwood Lumber Dispute and Canada - U.S. Trade in Natural Resources* Halifax, NS: The Institute for Research on Public Policy.

Perry, J. H.(1989). *A Fiscal History of Canada - The Postwar Years*, Toronto: Canadian Tax Foundation.

Plourde, Andre (1986). *Oil and gas in Canada: A chronology of important developments, 1941 - 1986*, (Policy and Economic Analysis Program, Energy Study No. 86-5), Toronto: Institute for Policy Analysis.

Postner, Harry H. & Leslie Wesa ((1985). *Employment instability in Western Canada: A diversification analysis of the manufacturing and other sectors* (Economic Council of Canada, Discussion Paper No. 275).

Rhomberg, Rudolf (1976). *Indices of effective exchange rates* (International Monetary Fund Staff Papers, Volume 23 pp 88-112). International Monetary Fund.

Rosensweig, J. A.(1987). "Constructing and using exchange rate indexes," *Federal Reserve Bank of Atlanta Economic Review* pp. 4-16.

Roussel, Phillip, Kamal Saad, & Tamara Erickson (1991). *Third Generation R&D*, Cambridge, MA: Harvard Business School Press.

Scarfe, Brian L (1987)."Canadian energy policy: A prospective view," in John G Rowse (Ed.),*World Energy Markets: Coping With Instability, Proceedings of the Ninth Annual Conference, International Association of Energy Economists*, (pp. 140-147). Calgary.

_____ (1985, Summer). "Canadian energy prospects: Natural gas, tar sands, and oil policy," *Contemporary Policy Issues III*(4), pp. 13-24.

_____, and Rilkoff, Edwin (1984) *Financing oil and gas exploration and development activity* (Discussion Paper No. 274), Ottawa: Economic Council of Canada.

Schott, Jeffrey (1988). *United States-Canada free trade: An evaluation of the agreement* Washington: Institute for International Economics.

Smith, R. S. (1990). *Spending and taxing: The recent record of Western Canadian provincial governments* (Information Bulletin No. 1) Edmonton: University of Alberta, Western Centre for Economic Research.

Ulrich, A., W. H. Furtan & A. Schmitz (1988). *The cost of a licensing system regulation: An example from Canadian prairie agriculture Journal of Political Economy*,95, 1, pp. 160-177.

Veeman, M. and T.S. Veeman (1985). *Western Canadian agriculture: Prospects, problems and policies* (Special Supplement) Toronto: *Canadian Public Policy* pp. 301-309.

Veeman, T. & M. S. Veeman (1984). *The future of grain: Canada's prospects for grains, oilseeds and related industries,* Toronto: Canadian Institute for Economic Policy (pp. 94-103).

Walker, Michael A.(1980). *Preface and Summary* In Michael A. Walker (Ed.),*Focus on Alberta's Industrial and Science Strategy Proposals* Vancouver: The Fraser Institute (pp. vii-xx).

Whalley, John, (Ed.),(1986). *Canada's resource industries* Toronto: University of Toronto Press and Ottawa: Minister of Supply and Services Canada.

Whalley, John and Irene Trela (1986). *Regional Aspects of Confederation* (Vol. 68 Research Studies) Toronto: Royal Commission on the Canadian Economic Union and Development Prospects.

Wigle, R.(1989). "Between a rock and a hard place: The economics of the Canada-U. S. freer trade," *Canadian Public Policy*, XV(2), pp. 145-161.

Wilkinson, Bruce W.(1987). *Canadian resource trade: An overview paper presented at the Third Banff Conference of Natural Resources Law: Trading Canada's Natural Resources*, Banff, Alberta.

_____ (1988). "The Saskatchewan potash industry and the 1987 antidumping action," *Canadian Public Policy* XIV(1), pp. 104-108.

_____(1989, Sept). *Regional trading blocks: the EC and Canada-U. S.* Unpublished memo.

World Bank (1986). *Price prospects for major primary commodities, Vol. I :summary and implications* Report No. 814/86 Washington, DC.

The Alberta Heritage Savings Trust Fund: An overview of the issues 1980, February), Canadian Public Policy (VI Supplement).

Commodity prices and Canada's resource sector, (1986, September), Bank of Canada Review, pp. 19-32.

Technical note: A weighted average exchange rate index for the Canadian dollar," (1984, September). *Bank of Canada Review* p. 19.

Western Canadian economic development: Energy policy and alternative strategies (1985, July), Canadian Public Policy (XI Supplement).

The Authors

Edward J. (Ted) Chambers
Dr. Ted Chambers is a Professor of Marketing and Economic Analysis in the Faculty of Business, and Director of the Western Centre for Economic Research at the University of Alberta. He has published in the areas of economic and business development, macroeconomics, and regional problems.

Michael B. Percy
Dr. Michael Percy is a Professor of Economics at the University of Alberta. He has published extensively in the areas of Canadian and regional economic development, resource management policies, and regional economic policy.